CONTROLS AND INFLATION

The Economic Stabilization Program in Retrospect

Marvin H. Kosters

In association with J. Dawson Ahalt

Foreword by George P. Shultz

American Enterprise Institute for Public Policy Research
Washington, D. C.

Marvin H. Kosters is a resident scholar at the American Enterprise Institute and former associate director for economic policy of the Cost of Living Council.

J. Dawson Ahalt is staff economist, Office of the Secretary, U.S. Department of Agriculture, and former deputy associate director for economic policy of the Cost of Living Council.

ISBN 0-8447-3177-3

Domestic Affairs Study 37, December 1975

Library of Congress Catalog Card No. 75-34688

Printed in the United States of America

CONTENTS

LIST OF TABLES

LIST OF FIGURES

ACKNOWLEDGMENTS

This review of the Economic Stabilization Program was prepared while the principal author was a resident scholar at the American Enterprise Institute for Public Policy Research. It draws heavily on the files of the Cost of Living Council and on files put together while I was associate director for economic policy and planning during almost the entire period of the stabilization program. J. Dawson Ahalt, who was deputy associate director for economic policy, prepared the initial draft of the food, lumber, fertilizer and hides sections of the paper while he was staff economist, agricultural economics, Office of the Secretary, U.S. Department of Agriculture. While overall responsibility for the study is mine, Dawson Ahalt made important contributions to the entire manuscript.

This review was initially presented at the Conference on Research in Income and Wealth on "Price Behavior, 1965–1974," sponsored by the National Bureau of Economic Research, held 21 through 23 November 1974 in Bethesda, Maryland. The paper is also scheduled to be published later by the National Bureau of Economic Research along with the related papers in a volume containing the proceedings of the conference. We gratefully acknowledge the special permission granted by the National Bureau of Economic Research for publication of this paper at this time.

We also gratefully acknowledge the support for the preparation of the paper by the National Science Foundation under grant number GS-43757, the Ford Foundation under grant number 740-0510, and the American Enterprise Institute for Public Policy Research.

The views expressed in this study are those of the authors and do not necessarily reflect the views of the organizations that contributed to the support of the research or with which the authors are affiliated.

Many helpful comments and discussions contributed materially to improving the study. Those whose assistance is acknowledged include John Dunlop, Kenneth Fedor, Joseph Burns, Yale Brozen, Dan Larkins, and Robert Aaron Gordon (who summarized and criticized the paper presented at the National Bureau of Economic Research conference). Janet Bollen assisted in obtaining data and was responsible for checking many of the computations and sources. I am also indebted to Phyllis Luther who typed successive drafts of the paper and who also assembled, organized, and drew upon my files, both at the Cost of Living Council and at the American Enterprise Institute, with diligence, competence, and consistent good humor.

Finally, I am indebted to my wife, Bonnie, and three children for their willingness to tolerate my long hours at work while I was at the Cost of Living Council and while the paper was being prepared.

FOREWORD

Those readers interested in a quick summary of this useful perspective on the relationship of controls and inflation can turn to the final chapter. Those who are really in a hurry, however, may just refer to Table 9. Here can be seen the movement in the price indexes from a time two-and-one-half years preceding the Economic Stabilization Program through the eight months following its demise. Its nineteen rows constitute the components of the price indexes, while its nine columns divide the total period into natural time segments.

At a glance one can see the overall trends, including the fact that only in one of the two short freeze periods was the increase in consumer prices less than the increase during the eight months of 1971 prior to the freeze. Great variability among sectors of the economy is evident throughout the entire period of the Economic Stabilization Program. Nowhere is this variability greater than during Phase III, where it can be seen that influences outside the scope of the program led to a rate of increase in prices which in turn undermined confidence in the program. Food and energy prices, essentially internationally traded commodities not subject to controls, increased by 20 percent and 18 percent, respectively, while nonfood commodities and services increased by 4.6 percent and 4.3 percent, respectively. Five or ten minutes spent scanning down the columns and across the rows of this table will yield other insights to the reader and suggest questions, many of which are dealt with in the text.

Several themes woven through this volume stand out in my mind and should be useful both to the analyst of this period of our economic history and to anyone considering installing and administering a controls program in the future.

The first theme is the virtual inevitability of stages during any lengthy controls program, despite the fact that the underlying approach of the program may remain almost the same. Thus, the changing administrative structure of the Economic Stabilization Program was built upon a relatively constant set of concepts involving such things as the pass-through of costs, with adaptations of dollar-for-dollar and percentage approaches, profit-margin comparisons with various base periods, industry and size-of-firm approaches to coverage, various averaging techniques for judging price changes, and so on.

Much more visible to the public and to those subjected to the controls mechanisms were the various administrative phases of the program. The shift from one phase to another has, in retrospect, received a fair amount of criticism as reflecting a kind of administrative uncertainty about the whole process. But, the perspective in this study suggests the inevitability of changes in administrative structure. This is particularly true when controls are seen as a temporary phenomenon but would be true as well if "phase out" were not the ultimate goal. Even a cursory study of experience with controls during World War II or the Korean War bears this point out. The dynamics of the initial freeze demanded a comprehensive follow-on structure. This structure was inevitably modified both in formal administrative setup and in the extent of self-administration in the whole process.

To a degree this "phasing" was going on virtually all the time, with only the more dramatic changes singled out for explicit labeling. In any case, whatever the consistency of the program's underlying concepts, the evolution of the administrative structure will preoccupy those in charge of managing the controls.

A second and related point is the interplay between changing structural relationships in the economy and developments in the controls program itself. In part, this is a question of the force of traditional relationships which, when not in balance, assert themselves. The authors' analysis of the wage side of the program brings this point out clearly, as they trace through the implications of imbalances in wage relationships (Art Ross's "coercive comparisons") for permissible increases in particular cases. But, in general, the seeds of the problems that must be faced in the controls program, or for that matter in economic developments without a controls program, can usually be found in the history of the immediate past. At the same time, the controls program itself is the prisoner of a vast array of links among parts of the economy. Thus, price changes for fertilizer cannot be considered without also considering what is to be done about explosives, because common raw materials are used. Indeed, a controls program forcefully demonstrates the high degree to which our economy is a closely interrelated and interdependent system.

A third idea which is found in many parts of this study is the link between domestic and international markets and the implications of that link for the administration of any controls program. While we know in our minds that the American economy is closely related to the world economy, we realize in our gut the force of that point as a result of observing the controls program in action. At the outset, price increases for imported articles were accepted, since not to accept them would deny us access to the world market. But, as the program progressed, the implications of our having domestic prices that were lower than world prices for internationally traded commodities became more and more apparent. If world prices were not to be accepted, then controls on prices would inevitably become controls on international trade, specifically in the form of quantitative limitations on exports. In turn, the administrative, let alone the policy, implications of allocating goods to other countries on some basis other than the price system are chilling to contemplate. As an aside, it is worth noting that this procedure operates in reverse. With all the current discussions about commodity agreements of one kind or another, it is well to remember that international controls will as surely lead to domestic controls as domestic controls were leading to international controls.

Phase III gave self-administration a bad name, but undeservedly so. The authors bring out the fact that self-administration worked, in the sense that the sectors of the economy covered by it pretty well conformed to the rules set out for them. What upset the apple cart, as is now generally recognized, was a worldwide surge of inflation beyond the reach of the domestic controls program. This point is particularly worth emphasizing, since large elements of self-administration will be necessary should controls again be imposed. Otherwise, even a large administrative apparatus would be swamped.

One final point brought out in this manuscript but too often overlooked: controls almost inevitably have a major impact on other central economic policies, sometimes for good, but sometimes for ill of major proportions.

On the good side, the problems of controls stimulated an intensive and, one hopes, continuing examination of government policies that contribute to inflation. Administratively, those charged with concern over inflation were given new and powerful leverage against pernicious policies promoted through government by powerful but segmented interests. Thus, excessive set-asides in planting, compulsory empty backhauls, restricted carloading of certain commodities, or size standards for produce designed to curtail supply, and a myriad of such other things were brought into discussion, and, in many cases, important changes were made. This effort to demand an "inflation impact statement," implicit or explicit, yielded important results during the controls period and holds the prospect for positive contributions to public policy with or without an economic stabilization program. It would be highly worthwhile for this effort to be institutionalized on a continuing basis.

On the bad side are the inevitable consequences of controls for government policy toward aggregate demand. The frequently heard argument that "needed" fiscal and monetary stimulation will be possible if there is an "adequate incomes policy" is proof enough of the most pernicious aspect of controls. It suggests why controls or any reasonably formal incomes policy are likely to lead to more inflation and not to less. It gives the body politic the illusion that the problem of inflation has somehow been taken care of and that, therefore, stimulative policies not otherwise appropriate may safely be followed. This has been the road to real inflation, as Table 9 in this study suggests.

The authors of this book labored with great dedication in the vineyards of the Economic Stabilization Program. Their performance was uniformly thoughtful, constructive, and balanced. They were responsible for some first-class analysis as the program unfolded. Now, in helping us all to gain a better perspective on this episode in our economic history, they have once again produced first-class material.

George P. Shultz

INTRODUCTION

From 15 August 1971 to 30 April 1974 mandatory controls on wages and prices were a component of the economic stabilization policy of the U.S. government. This experiment with "incomes policy" was the first peacetime wage and price control program in the United States. During the period marked changes occurred in the economic and political environment, in the structure of the program, in the rigor with which controls were administered or were perceived to be administered, and in the rates of price change that emerged. The pace of economic activity ranged from the early stages of a slow cyclical recovery to an extraordinarily vigorous boom in demand, followed by a period of short supply of basic materials, particularly petroleum products, and sharply curtailed production growth. Consumer price inflation initially declined from an annual rate of slightly below 4 percent in the eight months preceding controls to approximately 3 percent during the first year of controls. But it rose to "double digit" rates of 11.5 percent in the eight months before controls were ended and to 12.2 percent in the eight months after controls were removed.

To assess the influence of controls as an economic policy tool only in terms of what happened to the inflation rate while they were in force would obviously be much too superficial. Price and wage trends occurring under controls are conditioned by the need to allow flexibility for adjustments in response to changes in the market environment, or to adapt the controls so as to contain pressures for significant departures from equilibrium and to keep resources in the channels from which price suppression threatens to divert them. During the period of controls, changes in overall demand levels were of central importance in the market environment, but changes in supply conditions for particular sectors originating from both domestic and foreign sources were also important.

The extent to which controls were intended to affect economic goals other than prices—goals such as output, employment, investment, and efficiency—is relevant in an evaluation of the effects of the controls. Other factors that form part of the context in which controls were administered and that should be taken into account in evaluating the controls are broader goals such as limited bureaucratic intervention in price decisions and collective bargaining, balance-of-payments goals, international trade and foreign policy interests, maintenance of a competitive industrial structure, and preservation of private incentives to promote innovation and efficiency. Finally, a comprehensive assessment of controls should also look at economic conditions and prospects prior to the imposition of controls and developments after they were terminated.

The analysis and discussion in this paper is oriented toward an assessment of controls as a temporary and supplementary "incomes policy" tool. The analysis will look at their possible marginal influence on inflation when they are administered with an emphasis on avoiding serious short-term market disruption and minimizing adverse long-term effects on the economy. Chapter 1 reviews the economic and political developments that preceded the imposition of controls. Chapter 2 looks at the design of the controls system and changes in the structure of the program. In Chapter 3, the consistency of wage and price behavior with the stabilization regulations is examined by analyzing aggregate data on wage, price, and profits developments. A more detailed analysis of the role of controls in major sectors of the economy is presented in Chapter 4. The fifth chapter explores the question of inefficiency and distortions attributable to controls, while some broad issues concerning the role and limitations of direct controls as a stabilization tool are addressed in Chapter 6. The conclusions of the study are briefly summarized in Chapter 7.

1
BACKGROUND

Initially, a policy of gradualism that became known as the "game plan" was put into effect to reverse the rise in the rate of inflation that occurred in the last half of the 1960s.[1] Rapid expansion of aggregate demand from 1964 through 1966 after a period of relatively stable prices had brought the unemployment rate down to well below 4 percent, a lower rate than had been experienced in the preceding decade. After a pause in 1967, aggregate demand surged again in 1968. By 1969 the unemployment rate was 3.5 percent, with real output growth tapering off and prices rising more rapidly than before.

The gradual slowdown in aggregate demand growth that began during 1969 was induced by a swing from a substantial deficit to a small surplus in the federal budget in fiscal year 1969 and a slower rate of monetary expansion during 1969. A somewhat less pronounced deceleration in monetary expansion (relative to inflation trends) had occurred during 1966 and had been followed in 1967 by a slowdown in demand growth, virtually stable unemployment, and a noticeable deceleration in inflation, mainly confined to food prices. This experience suggested the promise of a policy of gradually reducing demand growth to a rate that would create pressures for smaller instead of larger price increases, without increasing unemployment so much that persistence in such a policy path would become politically untenable.

Adjustments in the economy in response to stringent fiscal policy and slower monetary expansion were expected to run in the following sequence:[2] slower growth in total spending in the economy, slower

---

1 Paul W. McCracken, "The Game Plan for Economic Policy," *Proceedings of the American Statistical Association*, Business and Economic Section (New York, 19-22 August 1969), pp. 294-98.

2 See, for example, *Economic Report of the President, 1970* (Washington, D. C.: U.S. Government Printing Office, February 1970), pp. 25-27.

production growth, pressure on profit margins and slower employment growth, smaller wage increases, and finally lower price inflation. The calibration of federal policy instruments necessary to introduce an appropriate degree of disequilibrium and the lags in the process were interrelated and uncertain. It was essential to restrain total spending growth enough to set in motion an adjustment process that would lead to deceleration in price increases, but a longer-than-anticipated lag before prices began to decelerate would result in lower real output levels and higher unemployment than were intended.

By the end of 1970 inflation had proved to be more persistent than had been expected. As a result real output was lower and prices and unemployment were higher than the earlier official projections.[3] These conditions persisted during the first half of 1971, with relatively slow output growth in the second quarter after a rebound in the first quarter from the strike-depressed fourth quarter of 1970. During the first half of 1971 both wholesale prices and the private GNP deflator increased at rates roughly similar to those at which they increased in the previous two years, although consumer prices were increasing less rapidly. The unemployment rate hovered at 6 percent, up from 3.5 percent in 1969. There were no clear indications that unemployment would be reduced appreciably in the ensuing months through more rapid demand growth, and the evidence that inflation was subsiding was tenuous. Furthermore, the rate of price increase, particularly for wholesale prices of industrial commodities, remained high by the standards suggested by the experience of the early 1960s, and the worsening balance of payments was an ominous cloud on the horizon.

The Political Context

There were several indications that the game plan was being played in economic overtime by the beginning of 1971. Unemployment had reached a level that threatened to be politically damaging to the Nixon administration in the absence of firm prospects that it would recede. Public and congressional sentiment became increasingly unfavorable toward the explicitly noninterventionist policies of the administration and shifted toward a preference for direct action to restrain "excessive" wage and price increases.

---

[3] The disappointing performance and the questions that it raised about reasons for the slow response are illustrated in the *Economic Report of the President, 1971* (February 1971), p. 28 and p. 60ff.

These conditions provided a climate in which the Democratic Congress enacted legislation in August 1970 authorizing mandatory controls. Whether or not such authority was used, the legislation could be used to embarrass the President and his party.[4] Business attitudes were conditioned by two years in which profits were ground between the millstones of rapidly increasing labor costs and markets in which these costs could not readily be passed through by increasing prices. In October 1970 the Business Council criticized the lack of direct action on wages and prices, a criticism that was reaffirmed in the spring.[5] The Committee for Economic Development, another business group, issued a policy statement in November 1970 recommending establishment of a stabilization body to establish "broad norms" for wage and price behavior.[6] On the labor side, the AFL–CIO had taken a position in support of "equitable" controls if the President determined they were necessary and George Meany had stated his view that they were.[7] Also, within the federal government several high officials had proposed some form of incomes policy, the most prominent being Arthur Burns, who had become chairman of the Federal Reserve Board in 1970.[8]

Faced with these developments, the administration was increasingly on the defensive in maintaining its noninterventionist stance. In June 1970, the President established the National Commission on Productivity and the Regulations and Purchasing Review Board, and announced that periodic "inflation alerts" would be prepared by the Council of Economic Advisers. In January of 1971, the President directed the Cabinet Committee on Economic Policy to analyze conditions in the steel industry in the wake of announced price increases for some steel products. The Council of Economic Advisers was to report immediately to the committee any "exceptionally inflationary wage or price developments"[9] so that appropriate federal

4 See also Lloyd Ulman's discussion of this aspect of the politics of incomes policies in "Phase II in Context: Towards an Incomes Policy for Conservatives," *Incomes Policy: What Can We Learn From Europe?*, ed. Walter Galenson (Ithaca, N. Y.: New York State School of Industrial and Labor Relations, Cornell University, 1973), p. 92.

5 Arnold R. Weber, *In Pursuit of Price Stability* (Washington, D. C.: The Brookings Institution, 1973), p. 6.

6 *Further Weapons against Inflation* (Washington, D. C.: Committee for Economic Development, 1970).

7 Weber, *In Pursuit of Price Stability*, p. 5.

8 The most widely noted statement by Burns was the Pepperdine speech, "The Basis for Lasting Prosperity," address in the Pepperdine College Great Issues Series, Los Angeles, California, 7 December 1970.

9 *Economic Report of the President, 1971*, p. 82.

action could be considered. The Construction Industry Collective Bargaining Commission had been established in September 1969, and federal action had been taken to reduce construction spending and encourage training of more skilled construction labor, but there had been no relief during 1970 from increasingly large construction wage increases and the pressures they created for similar wage increases in other sectors. On 29 March 1971 the Construction Industry Stabilization Committee was established to place mandatory controls on construction wages. After a review of the economy by the administration in June, decisions were announced not to apply additional stimulus to demand and not to establish an incomes policy. These statements proved to be the last strong official reaffirmation of the game plan.[10] Larger trade deficits and the increased vulnerability of the dollar to massive conversion into other forms of reserves were added to continuing disappointing news on prices and production, triggering the President's dramatic announcement of the New Economic Policy on 15 August 1971.

Economic Conditions in Mid–1971

By mid–1971 the game plan had been successful in bringing about some elements in the sequence of adjustments envisioned for the process of reducing inflation.[11] Slower monetary expansion combined with fiscal policy restraint had reduced the growth of total spending, slowed production and employment growth, squeezed profits, and

[10] The extent to which the public dialogue on inflation had come to be focused on incomes policy and the defensive position in which this placed the administration is illustrated by a statement by Paul McCracken, chairman of the Council of Economic Advisers, that "we have now in effect many elements of what has come rather loosely to be called an incomes policy. We are now considering ways to make these elements more systematic and comprehensive, and to provide more adequately for their management." U.S. Congress, Joint Economic Committee, *The 1971 Economic Report of the President*, 92d Cong., 1st sess. (5, 9, 17, 18, and 19 February 1971), p. 9.

[11] For a detailed review of stabilization developments and policy in the period before the introduction of controls, see Phillip Cagan, Marten Estey, William Fellner, Charles E. McLure, Jr., and Thomas Gale Moore, *Economic Policy and Inflation in the Sixties* (Washington, D. C.: American Enterprise Institute, 1972). For examples of discussions raising questions about changes in the response of real output growth and inflation to aggregate demand changes, see Robert J. Gordon, "Inflation in Recession and Recovery," *Brookings Papers on Economic Activity*, no. 1 (Washington, D. C.: The Brookings Institution, 1971), pp. 105-58, and the following papers in *Brookings Papers on Economic Activity*, no. 2 (1971): Charles L. Schultze, "Has the Phillips Curve Shifted? Some Additional Evidence," pp. 452-67; William Fellner, "Phillips-type Approach or Acceleration?" pp. 469-83; Arthur Okun, "The Mirage of Steady Inflation," pp. 485-98; and Robert J. Gordon, "Steady Anticipated Inflation: Mirage or Oasis?" pp. 499-510.

stabilized or reduced the rate of price inflation. The game plan had succeeded in achieving the early stages of the disinflation process, but further reduction in inflation depended on a trend toward smaller labor cost increases that had not yet emerged. While wages in some sectors were increasing less rapidly than before, very large increases in other sectors kept average hourly labor costs increasing at a roughly stable rate.

These developments raise two issues concerning stabilization policy performance before and after controls were imposed. One is the extent to which the buildup of significant distortions in the wage structure contributed to a slower unfolding of the disinflation process than had been projected. The other is the extent to which improved balance in the wage structure and prospects for more rapid productivity growth pointed to the possibility of improved economic performance after 1971 with or without wage and price controls.

Wages and Collective Bargaining.[12] The unemployment rate rose from 3.5 percent in 1969 to about 6 percent in late 1970. However, reduced growth of demand in labor and product markets was not accompanied by smaller wage increases. Adjusted average hourly earnings for the private nonfarm sector rose by 6.7 percent in 1970 and 7.0 percent in 1971, indicating that wage rates were increasing more rapidly than they had when unemployment rates were lower. New first-year wage increases under collective bargaining agreements in manufacturing rose from an average of about 8 percent in 1969 to nearly 11 percent in 1971 even though the unemployment rate in manufacturing increased from 3.3 percent in 1969 to 6.8 percent in 1971.

Continuing large wage increases under new collective bargaining agreements negotiated in 1970 and 1971 had their roots in earlier trends in prices and other wages. Wages for workers covered by long-term wage contracts in the late 1960s were depressed relative to those of other workers who received wage increases that more quickly reflected the strong labor market demand and accelerating inflation that prevailed during this period. When long-term contracts expired, there were strong pressures to restore the relative wage positions of the workers they covered through heavily front-loaded new contracts, because the deterioration of their position in the wage structure had resulted primarily from an unanticipated increase in inflation.

12 For a more detailed discussion of wage structural developments discussed in this section, see Marvin Kosters, Kenneth Fedor, and Albert Eckstein, "Collective Bargaining and the Wage Structure," *Labor Law Journal*, vol. 24, no. 8 (August 1973), pp. 517-25.

The pattern of relatively small increases during the term of existing wage contracts is illustrated by data that show large first-year wage increases under major collective bargaining agreements compared to deferred wage increases, and deferred increases that were generally smaller than wage increases received by the average worker from 1968 through 1971 (Appendix Table A-1). A similar pattern is shown by data on wage increases for union and nonunion workers in manufacturing. These data show relatively small wage increases for union workers from 1965 through 1969 (Appendix Table A-2). The influence of long-term contracts on the wage structure during the period of rising inflation is also evident in average hourly earnings changes for industry sectors in which most workers were covered by long-term wage contracts.

Data on average wage increases in six major industry sectors in which most workers were covered by long-term collective bargaining agreements with common expiration dates show deterioration in the relative wage position of these workers during the term of their contracts (Table 1). These workers received smaller wage increases than were received by the average private nonfarm worker in the two contract periods shown for each industry between 1966 and 1971. When new agreements were negotiated, average wages in the sectors covered increased by more than average wage increases for private nonfarm workers. In other words, there was a tendency to compensate at the time of negotiation for smaller wage increases during the term of the previous contract. The data in Table 1 suggest that inflation-induced distortion in the wage structure created conditions leading to unusually large first-year wage increases in major union settlements, particularly in 1970 and 1971.[13] These large negotiated wage increases contributed directly to rapid increases in hourly labor costs and influenced wage changes for related workers, impeding any significant reduction in inflation in spite of considerable slack in labor and product markets.

Large first-year wage increases for the great number of workers covered by contracts expiring in 1970 and 1971 had a significant direct influence on overall hourly labor cost increases. Their total

[13] This analysis is an application of wage structural concepts to the particular inflationary conditions of the late 1960s and early 1970s. Wage structural concepts have been applied in many studies of wage determination under collective bargaining, with concepts in this closely related body of ideas called "wage contours" (Dunlop), "orbits of coercive comparison" (Ross), "wage constellations" (Harbison), and "neighboring strategic wage rates" (Bronfenbrenner and Holzman). See Martin Bronfenbrenner and Franklyn D. Holzman, "Survey of Inflation Theory," *American Economic Review*, vol. 53, no. 4 (September 1963), p. 618.

Table 1

AVERAGE HOURLY EARNINGS INCREASES FOR SELECTED INDUSTRIES COVERED BY LONG-TERM COLLECTIVE BARGAINING AGREEMENTS AND WAGE INCREASES UNDER COLLECTIVE BARGAINING AGREEMENTS IN MANUFACTURING

	Annual Percentage Change in Average Hourly Earnings					
	1966	1967	1968	1969	1970	1971
Private nonfarm	4.5	4.7	6.3	6.7	5.9	6.5
Rubber	3.4	5.6		4.7	5.4	
Autos	2.9	8.6		5.5	13.1	
Trucking	2.9	6.0		6.0	13.8	
Steel		1.1	6.0		3.5	11.9
Metal cans		3.4	10.0		4.2	11.5
Communications		3.2	9.4		3.4	14.7
Manufacturing only (collective bargaining agreements)						
First-year increases			7.0	7.9	8.1	10.9
Deferred wage increases			3.9	4.0	4.6	4.8

Note: Percentage changes in average hourly earnings were computed as percentage changes in the average from the preceding year, except for those of industry sectors for the year in which new contracts were negotiated. New contracts were negotiated in the rubber, auto, and trucking industries in 1967 and 1970 and in the steel, metal cans, and communications industries in 1968 and 1971. The percentage increase in average hourly earnings in those industries for years in which new contracts were negotiated was computed by comparing average wages for a six-month period after the new contract was negotiated with the average for the same six-month period a year earlier. The particular months chosen are shown in Marvin Kosters et al., "Collective Bargaining and the Wage Structure," *Labor Law Journal*, vol. 24, no. 8 (August 1973), p. 522, Table 3.

contribution to rising hourly labor costs, though difficult to quantify, was certainly much larger than the direct effects of the newly negotiated wage settlements. A major share of the unexpectedly slow decline in wage and price increases in 1970 and early 1971 could have resulted from this much more serious and pervasive pattern of distortion in the wage structure than had been previously experienced during a cyclical slowdown in the economy. Imbalances in the wage structure and the large "catch-up" wage increases in 1970 and 1971 that reduced these imbalances created a transitional lag in wage developments. The pervasiveness of these imbalances also suggests that it would have been extremely difficult to embark on an incomes policy that relied heavily on a simple numerical wage standard, because its credibility could not easily be maintained when pressures for large catch-up wage increases by major unions were so strong.

Productivity and Prices. Continued acceleration of new, first-year wage increases under major collective bargaining agreements occurred throughout the period 1969–71. Smaller wage increases did occur in some sectors, such as nonunion manufacturing establishments, in spite of the demonstration effect of large wage increases for major unions, but this was part of the process through which balance in the wage structure was restored. While the make-up of contributions to higher average hourly labor costs shifted markedly between 1969 and 1971, the rate at which average hourly labor costs were increasing remained roughly unchanged from 1968 through 1971.

Extraordinarily slow productivity growth in 1969 and 1970, though a normal cyclical development, was protracted by the depressing effect on real output growth of the sluggish response of wages and prices to demand restraint. Combined with continued large average hourly labor cost increases, this slow productivity growth produced extremely large increases in labor costs per unit of output. Slack demand in product markets kept businesses from fully recouping the labor cost increases so that profits declined markedly in both 1969 and 1970. Because unit labor cost increases were so large and accounted for such a large share of total costs, the decline in profits could not absorb them, and as a result large price increases continued.

There are several points worth noting here. Pressures for the restoration of balance in the wage structure delayed the arrival of smaller hourly labor cost increases. This delay, and its influence on prices, generated a short-term real output growth path that was lower than had been projected, reinforcing cyclically slow productivity growth and intensifying the pressure of costs on prices. The prevalence of these cost pressures led to a "cost-push" diagnosis of the malady and influenced the design of criteria for price adjustments under the ensuing controls. Slow productivity growth precluded normal increases in real wage and income levels, thereby intensifying pressures for large wage increases, while profits were squeezed to the point where significant increases could be expected in a balanced recovery.

The Outlook in Mid–1971. By mid–1971 conditions had been created for a period of better economic performance. Better performance would require enough strength in aggregate demand to increase the pace of economic activity and enough stability (or some continued decline) in inflation so that stronger demand would raise production and employment levels and would not be dissipated in larger price increases. Prospects were favorable for improved wage and price performance during the cyclical recovery.

On the labor cost side, the period had passed in which pressures for large wage increases under new collective bargaining agreements were most severe. Moreover, deferred wage increases built into existing contracts had stabilized (Figure 1). Deferred increases scheduled to go into effect for 1972 were estimated to be slightly lower than for 1971. While there were some contracts for which large wage increases could be expected—coal miners, railroad workers and longshoremen—the collective bargaining calendar for 1972 showed fewer workers scheduled to negotiate new agreements and fewer large pattern-setting wage situations than there had been in 1970 and 1971. Moreover, large wage increases were not generally necessary to attract or retain labor in view of the slack in labor markets.

Productivity growth prospects were also favorable during the cyclical recovery in production that was under way. Roughly stable (or even somewhat smaller) hourly labor cost increases combined with more rapid productivity growth could reduce unit labor cost increases, thereby making possible smaller price increases, rising real wages and incomes, and some recovery in profits (Figures 2 and 3). Depressed capacity utilization rates suggested ample room for expansion of production without resulting in supply conditions that would create pressure for price increases or generate shortages.[14]

Thus, there was a reasonable prospect for a cyclical rise in productivity growth that would permit real incomes and profits to rise and relieve pressures for large wage and price increases. Realization of this outcome was not assured, however. The trend in newly negotiated wage increases might have been slow to respond to improved balance in the wage structure. Expectations of continued inflation and of possible direct action to restrain inflation might have contributed to persistence in price increases. Expansionary aggregate demand policies might consequently have been disproportionately translated into inflation rather than into real output growth.

[14] In discussing labor cost, productivity and price prospects at a Cornell University conference held in April 1972, Lloyd Ulman recognized that these conditions were favorable for an apparently successful incomes policy: "Thus, the policy of restraint could be effective or appear to be effective (if the stimulus to expansion came from other quarters), even if it did not succeed in its conventional task of restraining wage settlements directly. This could be regarded as the Indian Rope Trick Theory of incomes policy." Ulman, "Phase II in Context," p. 91.

Figure 1

WAGE INCREASES UNDER MAJOR COLLECTIVE BARGAINING AGREEMENTS

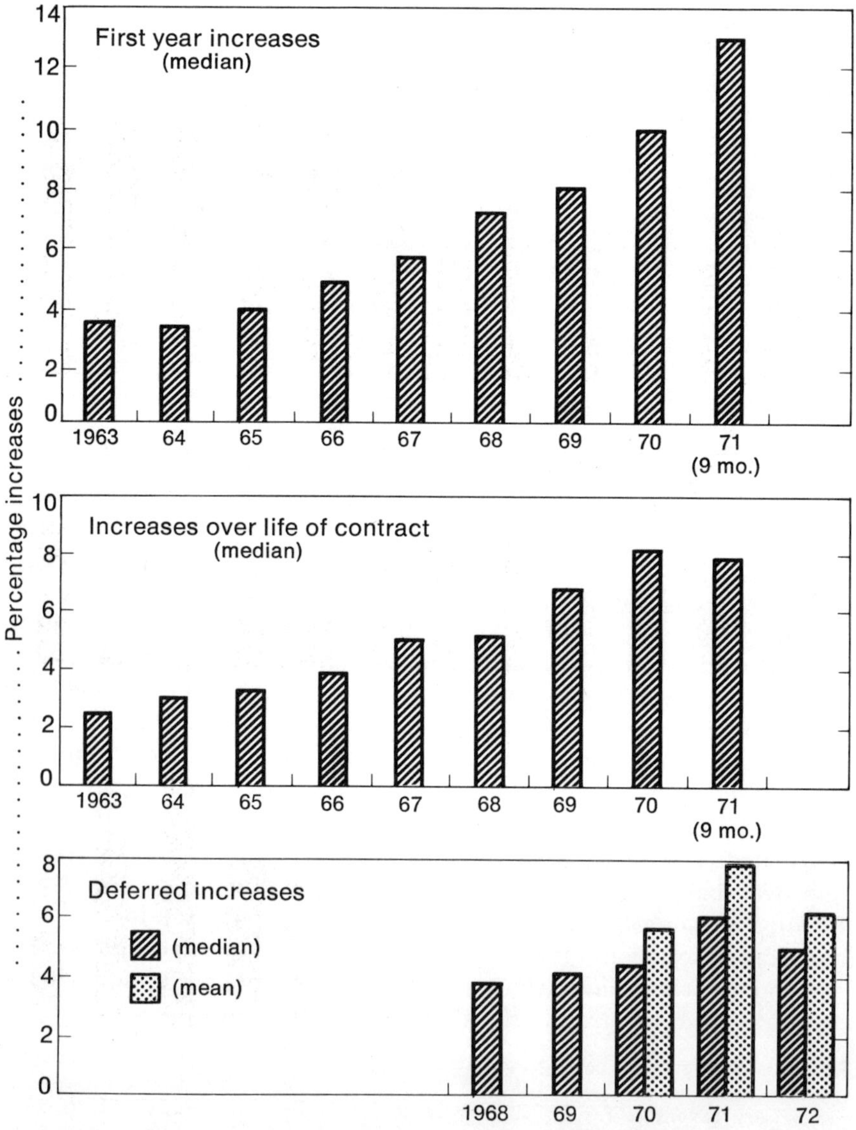

Note: These figures are for all industries and reflect wage increases only.
Source: U.S. Department of Labor, Bureau of Labor Statistics.

Figure 2

CHANGES IN PRODUCTIVITY, COMPENSATION, AND UNIT LABOR COSTS IN THE PRIVATE NONFARM ECONOMY, 1960–71

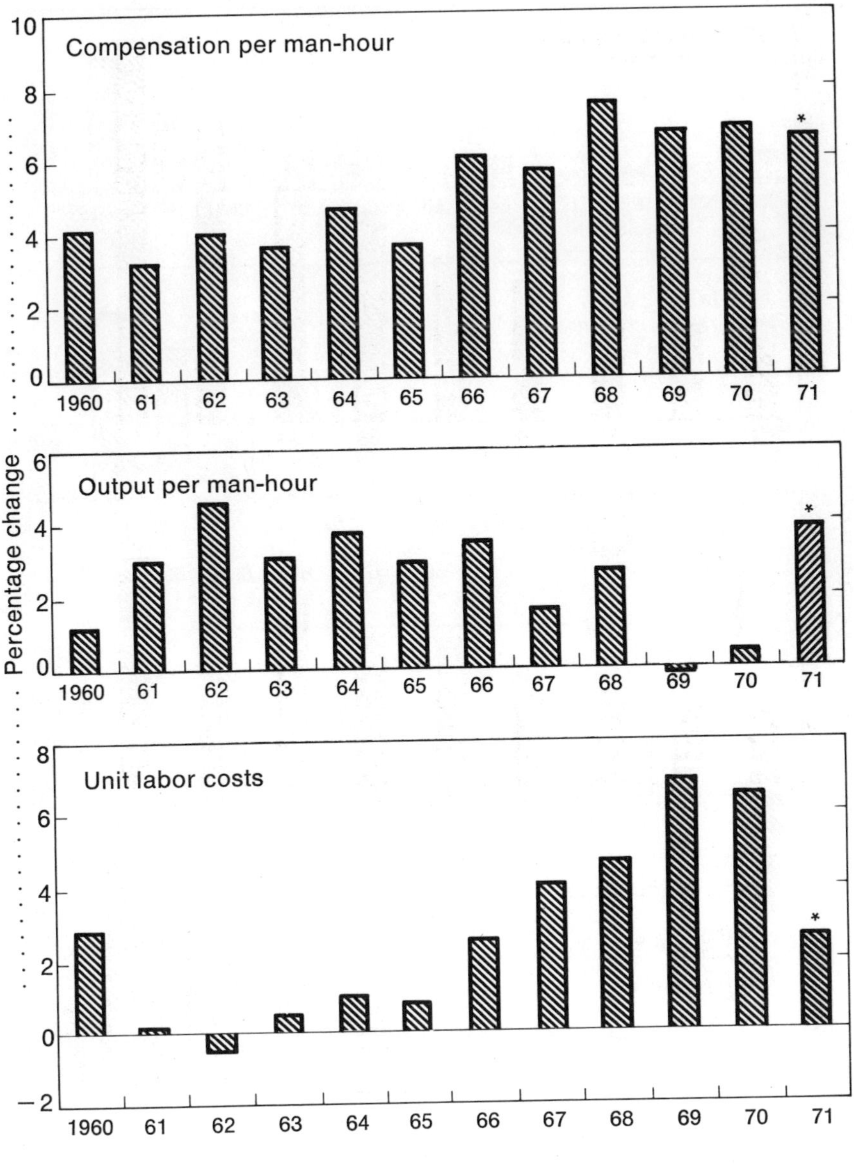

* First three quarters of 1971 over first three quarters of 1970.

Source: U.S. Department of Labor, Bureau of Labor Statistics.

Figure 3

CHANGES IN PRICES, LABOR COSTS, AND PROFITS FOR NONFINANCIAL CORPORATIONS, 1960–71

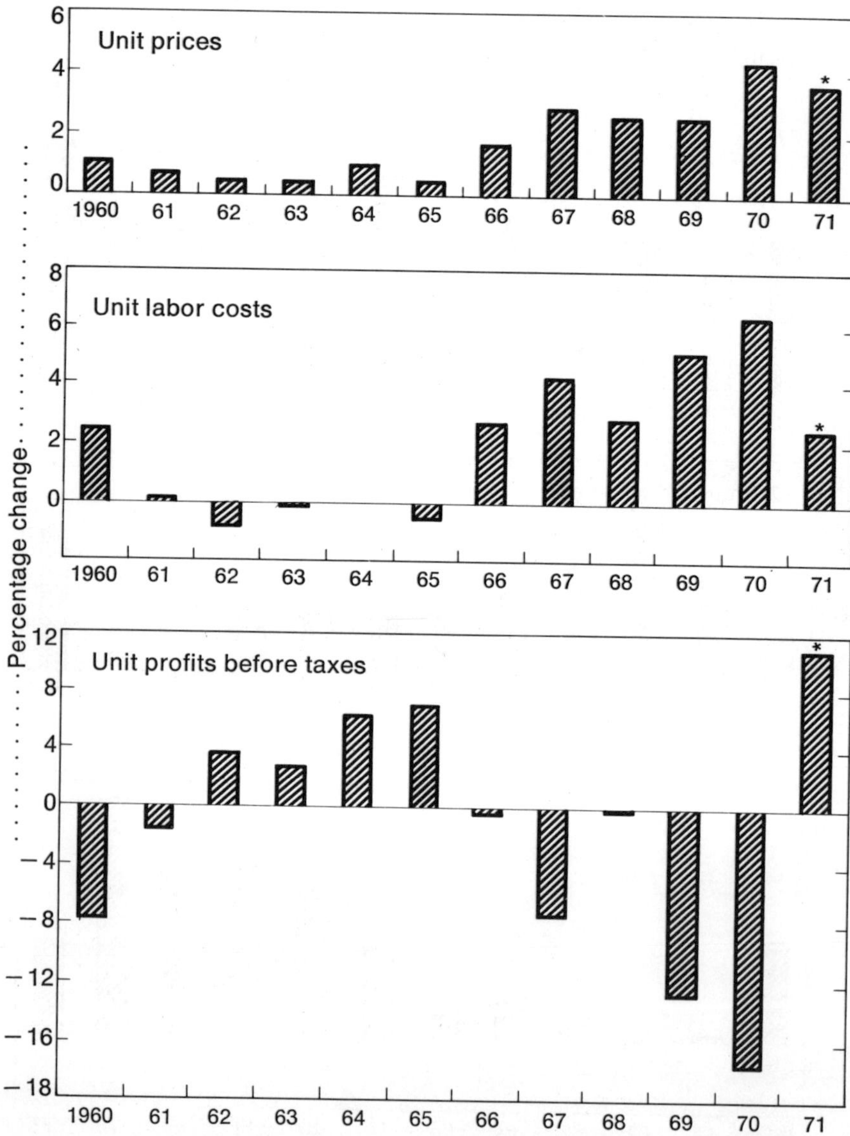

* First three quarters of 1971 over first three quarters of 1970.

Source: Department of Commerce, Bureau of Economic Analysis.

2 THE NEW ECONOMIC POLICY

The three elements of the New Economic Policy announced on 15 August 1971 were (1) suspension of dollar convertibility into gold and imposition of an import surcharge to deal with the balance-of-payments problem, (2) requests to Congress for an investment tax credit and other tax changes to stimulate output and employment, and (3) imposition of a ninety-day freeze on prices, wages, and rents. The New Economic Policy was motivated in large part by high unemployment and was triggered by the international situation—specifically an impending request for conversion of about $2 billion into gold. The element of the New Economic Policy with the most dramatic public impact was the freeze, even though the freeze and the system of controls that followed were intended as a short-term complement to the other policy changes and as a program to speed up the disinflation process that was already under way. The unexpected deterioration in price performance in 1973 meant, however, that extrication of most of the economy from controls was not completed until the authorizing legislation was allowed to expire on 30 April 1974.

Structure of the Controls

There were major changes in the organizational structure and administration of controls after the initial freeze and these changes were widely regarded as marked changes in controls policy. The conceptual basis for the regulations applicable to price and wage adjustments remained essentially unchanged, however, for most of the economy during the two and a half years from November 1971 through April 1974, except for the second brief freeze in mid–1973. Both regulations

Table 2

REGULATIONS OF THE CONTROLS PROGRAM, PHASES II, III, AND IV

Program	Phase II 14 November 1971 to 11 January 1973	Phase III 11 January 1973 to 13 June 1973	Phase IV 12 August 1973 to 30 April 1974
GENERAL STANDARDS			
Price increase limitations	Percentage pass-through of allowable cost increases since last price increase, or 1 Jan. 1971, adjusted for productivity and volume offsets. Term limit pricing option available.	Self-administered standards of Phase II.	In most manufacturing and service industries dollar-for-dollar pass-through of allowable cost increase since last fiscal quarter ending prior to 11 Jan. 1973.
Profit margin limitations	Not to exceed margins of the best 2 of 3 fiscal years before 15 Aug. 1971. Not applicable if prices were not increased above base level, or if firms "purified" themselves.	Not to exceed margins of the best 2 fiscal years completed after 15 Aug. 1968. No limitation if average price increase does not exceed 1.5 percent.	Same years as Phase III, except that a firm that has not charged a price for any item above its base price, or adjusted freeze price, whichever is higher, is not subject to the limitation.
Wage increase limitations	General standard of 5.5 percent. Exceptions made to correct gross inequities, and for workers whose pay had increased less than 7 percent a year for the last 3 years. Workers earning less than $2.75 per hour were exempt. Increases in qualified fringe benefits permitted raising standard to 6.2 percent.	General Phase II standard, self-administered. Some special limitations. More flexibility with respect to specific cases. Workers earning less than $3.50 per hour were exempted after 1 May.	Self-administered standards of Phase III. Executive compensation limited.

PRENOTIFICATION			
Prices	Prenotification required for all firms with annual sales above $100 million, 30 days before implementation, approval required.	After 2 May 1973, prenotification required for all firms with sales above $250 million whose price increase has exceeded a weighted average of 1.5 percent.	Same as Phase II except that prenotified price increases may be implemented in 30 days unless CLC requires otherwise.
Wages	For all increases of wages for units of 5,000 or more; for all increases above the standard regardless of the number of workers involved.	None.	None.
REPORTING			
Prices	Quarterly for firms with sales over $50 million.	Quarterly for firms with sales over $250 million.	Quarterly for firms with sales over $50 million.
Wages	Pay adjustments below standard for units greater than 1,000 persons.	Pay adjustments for units greater than 5,000 persons.	Same as Phase III.
SPECIAL AREAS	Health, insurance, rent, construction, public utilities.	Health, food, public utilities, construction, petroleum.	Health, food, petroleum, construction, insurance, executive and variable compensation.
EXEMPTIONS	Raw agricultural commodities, import prices, export prices, firms with 60 or fewer employees.	Same as Phase II plus rents.	Same as Phase III plus public utilities, lumber, copper scrap, and long-term coal contracts, initially with sector-by-sector decontrol of prices and wages until 30 April 1974.

Source: Cost of Living Council.

and procedures were modified over time, but the initial wage standard was not formally changed and the standards for price adjustments generally permitted costs to be passed through with profit margin limitations if prices were increased.

The broad outlines of the standards, procedures, and coverage of the program are summarized in Table 2. This material set forth in the table is amplified in the text by a discussion of some of the salient features of the program's organization and administration.[1] Some of the more detailed technical aspects of the rules and their practical effects are considered in later chapters.

Phase II

The Cost of Living Council established the price goals for the stabilization program, exercised authority over procedural issues and issues of coverage, coordinated policies and activities of the other stabilization bodies, and retained planning and policy development responsibility. The goal of reducing inflation to 2 to 3 percent by the end of 1972 was established to permit a gradual reduction in inflation (after an upsurge in the wake of the freeze) and to establish a context within which the Pay Board and Price Commission could develop and administer their standards. Raw agricultural products were the major sector exempt from controls, and coverage remained basically unchanged during the program, except for the small-firm exemption in May 1972 and the decontrol process in late 1973 and early 1974. A stabilization unit within the Internal Revenue Service was established to provide the field organization for the program and to conduct auditing and enforcement activities.[2]

---

[1] This study includes little discussion of Phase I, the wage-price freeze of 1971, which is the subject of a careful study by Arnold R. Weber, *In Pursuit of Price Stability*, cited earlier. Weber was director of the Cost of Living Council during the freeze and served as a public member of the Pay Board during Phase II.

A very brief and lucid sketch of the stabilization program is contained in John T. Dunlop, "Inflation and Incomes Policies: The Political Economy of Recent U.S. Experience," *Eighth Monash Economics Lecture* (Monash University, Australia, October 1974).

[2] The director of the Cost of Living Council was Donald Rumsfeld, who was also counselor to the President. The council was chaired by the secretary of the treasury, initially John B. Connally and beginning in the second quarter of 1972 George P. Shultz. In addition to the Pay Board and Price Commission, the Construction Industry Stabilization Committee was continued as an operating unit and the Committee on Interest and Dividends was established. In addition, three advisory committees were created: the Health Services Industry Committee, the Committee on State and Local Government Cooperation, and the Rent Advisory Board.

Phase II began on 14 November 1971. One of its distinguishing features was its heavy reliance on self-administration. The formal coverage of the standards was broader than the reach of administrative intervention through formal review of individual wage and price adjustments. A system of differentiated administrative procedures based primarily on size of firms and employee units was devised to reconcile broad coverage with limited administrative involvement. Administration of the controls was influenced in several ways by the administration's desire to minimize intrusion by a federal bureaucracy into price and wage decisions.

First, heavy reliance was placed on self-administration of the standards for smaller units; these units were subject only to periodic review or a small probability of possible audit. In this respect, the regulations were administered in a way similar to the way the personal income tax is administered. Second, the standards were designed to be generally applicable in order to permit self-administration, even though they were often difficult to apply to particular cases and inevitably much too simple to cover the full range of complex situations in the economy. Third, the regulations were applied to individual firms or employee units with relatively little consideration for industry price patterns and cost patterns or for wage patterns among industries, crafts, and occupations. These characterizations apply with particular force for Phase II. A more varied and complex approach was evolved beginning in 1973, reflecting changes in market conditions and an increased recognition of the inappropriateness of such a simplified approach over time.

Wages. A general numerical standard for wage increases was established, permitting compensation adjustments of up to 5.5 percent without prior notification or review for all except the largest employee units. Although criteria for exceptions were also provided, the wide applicability of the standard left little scope for adjustments in the wage structure. The intellectual roots of this approach can be traced to the rationale for the guideposts of the early 1960s. Its public acceptability as a credible approach owed much to widespread public discussion of the potential contribution of a general numerical norm for wage increases.[3] Moreover, it was compatible with an emphasis

[3] The guideposts outlined in the 1962 *Economic Report* were put forward as a contribution to public discussion, and the impact on public attitudes of widespread discussion of the concept may be illustrated by the opening sentence of the policy statement adopted by the Pay Board on 8 November 1971 establishing the general standard: "Millions of workers in the Nation are looking to the Pay Board for guidance with respect to permissible changes in wages. . . ." It may also be illustrated by the reaction of the press to the statement of the

on self-administration. Under the wage standard, wages and fringe benefits were treated as perfect substitutes. This treatment was consistent with an emphasis on the cost implications of pay adjustments, but it complicated the treatment of situations in which large fringe benefit increases were at issue.[4]

While differential procedural treatment for wage adjustments was formally based on employee-unit size, in practice the review and formal approval of pay adjustments was restricted largely to increases that exceeded the general standard with self-administration generally applicable to increases within the limits of the standard. Although the pay standard was widely viewed by the public as setting a limit of 5.5 percent (later recognized to be 6.2 percent under provisions dealing with fringe benefits), the actual standard and the way it was administered were more complex. Pay increases of up to 7 percent were permitted for deferred wage increases and as exceptions for tandem relationships, for "catch-up" to offset relatively small previous wage increases and for retaining essential employees. Increases exceeding those explicitly permitted by the regulations could be and were often permitted after review of a particular case.[5]

The regulations covering wage increases were initially developed and administered by a tripartite Pay Board.[6] After four of the five original labor representatives withdrew their participation on 22 March 1972, the Pay Board was reconstituted as a public body with seven members. While a measure of underlying labor cooperation and acquiescence was retained throughout Phase II, organized labor's formal participation in the program was not renewed until the advent of Phase III. Labor participation at a policy level instead of an

---

Labor-Management Advisory Committee of 26 February 1973 stating that "no single standard or wage settlement can be equally applicable at one time to all parties in an economy so large, decentralized and dynamic." See, for example, "The Magic Number Is a Blur," *New York Times*, 4 March 1973, and Edward Cowan, "Hocus-Pocus on Wage Guidelines," *New York Times*, 11 March 1973.

[4] Later in 1972, in response to an amendment to the Economic Stabilization Act, provision was made for larger than previously permitted pay increases to reflect introduction of improvements in "qualified fringe benefits"—mainly pensions. The coal settlement, the first case reviewed by the Pay Board, included a large increase in labor costs that was necessary to assure the solvency of the pension fund. It provides an example of how wage issues are complicated by circumstances unique to the situation under review.

[5] For a perceptive discussion of problems in the administration of wage controls and the emphasis that was placed on a general standard with few exceptions, see Arnold R. Weber, "Making Wage Controls Work," *The Public Interest*, no. 30 (Winter 1973), pp. 28-40.

[6] The chairman of the Pay Board was George H. Boldt, and the board was initially composed of fifteen members—five representing the general public, five representing business, and five representing labor.

operating level was obtained through establishment of the Labor-Management Advisory Committee, and a significant impetus for restructuring the program in Phase III came from a recognition that a participatory and cooperative role for labor was essential for any program of wage and price restraint.

Prices. The pricing standards for Phase II were developed and administered by the Price Commission.[7] Price adjustments were permitted if there had been cost increases, subject to the provision that these price increases did not lead to profit margins that exceeded limits established by a base period. Both the cost pass-through and profit margin rules were applied on a firm-by-firm basis, an approach that made self-administration feasible. All firms except the largest could apply the regulations themselves in making price adjustments. The largest firms had to submit requests for price increases and secure approval before those increases could be put into effect. For retail and wholesale operations the cost pass-through regulations permitted maintenance of percentage markups on the cost of merchandise only, while in the manufacturing and services sectors increases in all allowable costs incurred could be passed through on a percentage basis. Price increases to reflect increased merchandise costs for retailers and wholesalers were self-administered even in the largest firms, as were price adjustments for producers of products for which major input costs were exceptionally volatile—for example, in meat-packing operations. More specialized rules, also based on cost pass-through concepts, were developed for health services, insurance, and rents.

The Shift to Phase III

The restructuring of the stabilization program for Phase III was designed to provide a way station out of controls and to secure renewed cooperation in a program of wage and price restraint. From the time they were initially imposed, wage and price controls had been viewed by the administration as a short-term approach. It was repeatedly announced that the goal was to terminate controls as soon as this was feasible.[8] Phase III was intended to be a transitional stage

[7] The chairman of the Price Commission, composed of seven public members, was C. Jackson Grayson.

[8] See, for example, the President's address announcing the freeze, and "Background for the Post-freeze Economic Stabilization Program," Cost of Living Council, 7 October 1971.

in the process of removing mandatory wage and price controls. At the same time it was intended to contribute toward continued restraint. One element in this restraint involved enlisting the cooperation of organized labor during a year in which the bargaining calendar was heavy and a resurgence of large wage increases regarded as likely by many observers.[9] The other major element involved special attention to sectors in which continuing inflation problems were regarded as most severe, not only through the application of specialized controls mechanisms but also by an emphasis on federal policies influencing supply, particularly in the agricultural sector. How much Phase III contributed to restraint is a complex problem, but it clearly failed as an attempt to remove controls. Its demise came with the imposition of a new price freeze after five months of retreat from flexibility and self-administration.

The major organizational changes in Phase III were the termination of the Pay Board and Price Commission and the assumption of operational responsibility by the Cost of Living Council.[10] New committee structures were formed for the food and health sectors (an advisory committee with private sector representatives and a government committee to review federal policies influencing inflation for each sector) while the Construction Industry Stabilization Committee continued to operate. Standards and procedures in these three sectors continued basically unchanged from what they were in Phase II.

For other sectors of the economy the major substantive changes in the program were a modification of the price standard and a change in the administration of price and wage standards. The price standard was modified so as to reduce the constraining influence of profit margin limitations; the profit margin limitation was removed for firms with cost-justified price increases averaging less than 1.5 percent, and the base period that could be used in computing the profit margin limits was extended forward to the most recently completed fiscal year. Prenotification requirements for wages and prices were terminated, although quarterly reports were required for the largest units. Moreover, broad conformance with the standards was required instead

[9] See Don R. Conlan, "1973 U.S. Economic Outlook," *New York Times*, 3 September 1972, and the editorial, "Phase III Controls: Too Vague, Too Narrow, Too Weak," in *Business Week*, 10 March 1973, in which labor leaders were said to be "openly scornful of the idea that wage increases can be held to the 5.5% guideline of Phase II."

[10] John T. Dunlop became the director of the Cost of Living Council when Phase III was introduced. He had been chairman of the Construction Industry Stabilization Committee since its inception.

of detailed technical compliance with regulations, since detailed technical compliance would need to be accompanied by increasing complexity and detail in the regulations and carefully spelled-out rulings for particular situations. These changes toward "voluntary" and "self-administered" standards were perhaps of most substantive importance and generated most public interest.

On the wage side, the new director affirmed as one of his guiding principles the statement by the Labor-Management Advisory Committee that "no single standard or wage settlement can be equally applicable at one time to all parties in an economy so large, decentralized, and dynamic." [11] Although the change in emphasis was widely viewed as a repudiation of the wage norm for Phase II, the main practical effect of the change was to give more explicit attention to wage structural relationships and patterns but not to raise the average level of wage settlements.[12] On the price side, one of the most revealing indications of the direction in which the program was oriented was the clause in the general price standard permitting adjustments that would otherwise exceed the standards "as necessary for efficient allocation of resources or to maintain adequate levels of supply." Apart from the unwinding of delays that had previously been introduced by prenotification requirements, there was little formal change in the substance of the regulations, however, because the regulations, computational procedures, and rulings developed in Phase II were to be used in self-administering adjustments in both prices and wages.

The development and introduction of Phase III had been premised on a view of the price outlook that was far more optimistic than the inflation trend that actually emerged—a failure in prediction that was shared by most professional forecasters.[13] It was also based on

[11] Statement of the Labor-Management Advisory Committee, 26 February 1973, reprinted as Appendix G of *Statement by Dr. John T. Dunlop*, director, Cost of Living Council, before the Subcommittee on Production and Stabilization of the Senate Committee on Banking, Housing, and Urban Affairs, 6 February 1974, p. A-67. Dr. Dunlop's entire statement is reprinted in *Economic Stabilization Program Quarterly Report* covering the period 1 January 1974 through 1 May 1974 (Washington, D. C.: U.S. Government Printing Office, 1974), pp. 129-381, and in U.S. Congress, Senate Committee on Banking, Housing, and Urban Affairs, Subcommittee on Production and Stabilization, *Hearings: Oversight on Economic Stabilization*, 93d Cong., 2d sess. (30 and 31 January, 1 and 6 February 1974), pp. 445-667.

[12] Tripartite committees were established to review wage adjustments in the food industry and the health services sector where self-administration was not permitted.

[13] See Appendix A of the *Statement of Dr. John T. Dunlop*, p. A-1, in which a large number of inflation projections for 1973 are tabulated. The actual rise in

the view that the combination of substantive economic conditions in the labor market (particularly the restoration of improved balance in the wage structure) and the cooperative involvement of organized labor in a program to maintain stability made wage restraint during the year a realistic and achievable objective. Wage increases during 1973 were reasonably consistent with prospects as they were viewed in late 1972, in spite of price increases much larger than had been projected.[14]

The surge in food prices, led by large increases in meat prices, began in December 1972. By the end of March, ceilings were imposed on meat prices, based on the expectation at that time that food prices would rise less rapidly later in the year and the view that temporary meat price ceilings could therefore help to maintain restraint in wage settlements. At the beginning of May, the acceleration of price increases had become much broader and limited prenotification was reinstituted to introduce some delay in the pass-through of increased costs of a wide range of basic materials. By June the earlier optimism regarding food prices later in the year was no longer tenable, and accelerating price increases had become more pervasive throughout the economy. The widespread perception that Phase III was a failure and that a return to a controls structure similar to Phase II could contribute to renewed stability undoubtedly influenced public and congressional attitudes. The decision to terminate Phase III was the policy response.

The sharp acceleration of price increases in 1973 coincided closely in timing with the shift to Phase III but owed little to modifications in the standards of Phase II and their administration. Perhaps the strongest evidence that the shift to Phase III was not responsible for the acceleration is the fact that the acceleration began in food prices and food prices remained the major contributor to higher living costs through most of the year—even though mandatory controls on food prices, including prenotification requirements, were retained throughout Phase III. Moreover, price increases in most other sectors were supported by increased costs (according to the quarterly reports covering the period), most of the largest price increases were within

---

the GNP deflator was over 5 percent while most projections were between 3 and 4 percent. The difference between the actual and projected rise in consumer prices was even larger because food prices rose much more rapidly than most other prices, and food accounts for a larger share of the consumer price index than it accounts for in the GNP deflator.

[14] For a statement on the administration's view of the wage outlook, see statement of George P. Shultz, secretary of the treasury and chairman, Cost of Living Council, on 29 January 1973 in U.S. Congress, Senate Committee on Banking, Housing and Urban Affairs, *Hearings on S. 398: A Bill to Extend and Amend the Economic Stabilization Act of 1970*, 93d Cong., 1st sess. (1973), pp. 11-12.

the limits permissible during Phase II, and profits and cost data from other sources show no sharp break with earlier trends. Taken together, this evidence indicates that the problem was not a failure of compliance with the cost pass-through regulations that had been in force since the program began. Consequently, the principal action tool of Phase III, the "stick in the closet" to induce compliance, turned out to be highly inappropriate as an instrument for tempering the kind of inflation that emerged.

Freeze II and Phase IV

The public dialogue on inflation during the first half of 1973 was dominated by discussion of controls and their apparent lack of stringency. In this climate public and congressional pressures rose for strong direct action. A price freeze announced 13 June 1973 was a response to these pressures, despite economic judgments that its disruptive consequences would outweigh its contribution to price stability. The duration of the freeze was not to exceed sixty days; it covered only prices, with wages to be adjusted under existing standards and procedures; and it was to be followed by a stringent program of controls. It was lifted on a sectoral basis as sectors were placed under regulations similar to but somewhat more stringent than those of Phase II, beginning 18 July with the food sector, where market disruptions were most severe. The introduction of Phase IV was also accompanied by announced intentions to decontrol on a sector-by-sector basis.

The standards of Phase IV generally permitted pass-through of increased costs, although there was more differentiation among sectors in the application of this principle. Costs could only be passed through on a dollar-for-dollar basis, however, which had not been the case in Phase II, and prices in a number of sectors were significantly limited since further increases in prices were restricted to increases in costs occurring since the last quarter of 1972 that had not been reflected by price increases during that period. While situations in which the price ceilings of Phase IV held prices below market levels were far more numerous than situations in which the price ceilings had suppressed them in earlier phases, this was mostly attributable to changes in both domestic and world market conditions, to more use of delays in sectors such as steel, and to specialized sectoral regulations, particularly in the petroleum, health, and food sectors.

The difference between 1972 and 1973 market conditions and the extent to which the actual trend of consumer prices during the year would depend on decisions and developments wholly unrelated to controls is illustrated by two areas singled out by the President in his announcement of the freeze—gasoline and food prices. In the announcement he referred to strong export demand for farm products, and requested from the Congress more flexible authority for export controls. Comprehensive export controls for farm products were not imposed, because it was recognized that their imposition would seriously compromise other goals. However, stabilization of food prices at retail was inconsistent with a dramatically rising cost structure that reflected the rise of raw farm product prices on world markets. While the full implications of rising crude oil prices were not evident at this time, prices on world markets were rising above domestic levels well before the embargo, and the U.S. economy was dependent on supplies from foreign sources. Controls could and did play a role in keeping petroleum product prices below levels they would otherwise have reached, but there was no escape from the significant price consequences of the tripling of imported crude oil prices late in the year.

Although the Phase IV regulations were substantively similar for most sectors to those that had been in force in Phase II, the general policy approach that was followed differed in two fundamental ways. There was less reluctance to tolerate temporary dislocations resulting from the controls, such as dispersion in domestic prices and instances of domestic prices below prices on international markets. These conditions had been mainly confined to the lumber industry during Phase II. Though they were more prevalent and more severe during Phase IV, remedial adjustments were usually not made unless it could be demonstrated that these conditions would have seriously harmful and costly effects. At the same time, initiatives for the selective decontrol of individual sectors were carried forward, gradually at first and at a faster pace in early 1974. Criteria for decontrol and its timing were never publicly set forth in detail, but they frequently involved commitments from industry representatives with respect to prices, investment, or improvement of industrial relations practices.[15] This approach helped to avoid a disorderly retreat from

[15] Commitments of some form were made in connection with decontrol for a total of eighteen industry sectors. See *Economic Stabilization Program Quarterly Report* covering the period 1 January 1974 through 1 May 1974, chap. 2, pp. 13-70, and "Removing Controls: The Policy of Selective Decontrol," *Historical Working Papers on the Economic Stabilization Program*, Part 2 (Washington, D. C.: U.S. Government Printing Office, 1974), pp. 859-948.

controls through administrative breakdown or overwhelming pressures from litigation or from congressional initiatives. At the same time the continuing pinch of controls kept counterpressures against decontrol from building.

The elements of the decontrol process are not easily summarized, but it was oriented toward an orderly and cumulative extrication from controls. One of its guiding principles was a general policy of decontrolling both wages and prices in each case. The somewhat paradoxical role played by price prospects is illustrated on the one hand by decontrol of lumber when Phase IV began because prices were declining, and on the other by early decontrol of fertilizer in spite of large price increases because decontrol would contribute to increased domestic supply. The administration's position on extension of the stabilization authority was also designed to facilitate continued decontrol while retaining enough flexibility to promote effective dialogue among private sector interests, the Congress, and the executive branch. By 30 April 1974, more than half of the portion of the economy covered when Phase IV began had been decontrolled, with only 12 percent of the consumer price index remaining under control as against 44 percent before decontrol began. Congressional attitudes had changed so markedly from the previous year that no action was taken to provide for the limited mandatory authority requested by the administration, or even to establish a basis for monitoring the private sector and for analysis and policy review within the executive branch explicitly directed toward longer-term inflation concerns.[16]

---

[16] See John T. Dunlop, "Toward a Less Inflationary Society" (Remarks to the Society of American Business Writers, San Francisco, 6 May 1974) in *Economic Stabilization Program Quarterly Report* covering the period 1 January 1974 through 1 May 1974, pp. 599-607, for a discussion of areas in which federal government initiatives could make a contribution to reducing inflation.

3
CONTROLS AND THE ECONOMY

The effects of controls on the economy, and the effects of developments in the economy on controls, can be approached from various points of view. Each approach can give insight into some aspect of the relation between stabilization actions and economic goals, but regardless of the approach the insights cannot be easily summed up to provide an overall assessment. Careful analyses using different approaches have supported different conclusions on the influence of controls on wages, prices, and profits during the program.[1] In this chapter, the stabilization program is examined primarily from the point of view of overall consistency of performance with the stabilization rules.

General Performance of the Economy

Wage and price controls were only one component of economic policy during the period from 1971 through 1974, and improved price stability was one of several goals of economic policy in that period. Controls and their administration were regarded as closely linked with the high priority goal of a vigorous cyclical recovery in 1972.

---

[1] See, for example, Robert J. Gordon, "The Response of Wages and Prices to the First Two Years of Controls," *Brookings Papers on Economic Activity*, no. 3 (Washington, D. C.: The Brookings Institution, 1973), pp. 765-78, and William D. Nordhaus, "The Falling Share of Profits," *Brookings Papers on Economic Activity*, no. 1 (Washington, D. C.: The Brookings Institution, 1974), pp. 169-208. See also Daniel J. B. Mitchell, "Phase II Wage Controls," *Industrial and Labor Relations Review*, vol. 27 (April 1974), pp. 351-75; Michael Wachter, "Phase II, Cost-Push Inflation and Relative Wages," *American Economic Review*, vol. 64 (June 1974), pp. 482-91; Edgar Feige and Douglas Pearce, "The Wage-Price Control Experiment—Did It Work?" *Challenge*, vol. 16 (July/August 1973), pp. 40-44.

Table 3

EMPLOYMENT AND PRODUCTION CHANGES IN THE U.S. ECONOMY, 1969–73, AND AVERAGE FOR PRECEDING DECADE

	Average for 1959–69	1969	1970	1971	1972	1973
Employment						
Total civilian employment (millions)	70.2	77.9	78.6	79.1	81.7	84.4
Change in employment (millions)	1.3	1.9	0.7	0.5	2.6	2.7
Unemployment rate (percent)	4.8	3.5	4.9	5.9	5.6	4.9
Production (percentage change in constant dollars)						
Gross national product	4.3	2.7	−0.4	3.3	6.2	5.9
Private nonfarm output	4.5	2.8	−0.6	3.5	7.1	6.2

Source: U.S. Department of Labor, Bureau of Labor Statistics, and *Economic Report of the President, 1975* (Washington, D. C.: U.S. Government Printing Office, February 1975), p. 251.

Their influence on this goal was initially uncertain and given close attention.[2]

That controls did not interfere with a resumption of strong cyclical growth and may have contributed to it is an assertion that needs little qualification. Real output rose by about 6 percent in both 1972 and 1973 compared to 3.3 percent in 1971, the first year of the recovery. Although the unemployment rate declined only gradually throughout 1972 and 1973, increases in employment and in the labor force were unusually large. Employment rose by more than 2.5 million workers in 1972 and 1973 compared to an annual average rise of 1.3 million between 1959 and 1969 (Table 3). The

[2] See, for example, Milton Friedman's discussion of this question in his *Newsweek* column of 8 November 1971. Reprinted in Milton Friedman, *An Economist's Protest* (Glen Ridge, New Jersey: Thomas Horton and Company, 1972), pp. 20-22.

period of rapid increase in output that extended through the first quarter of 1973 was accompanied by strong cyclical productivity growth, a short-term development that contributed heavily to the favorable price, income, and profits trends of 1972 (Table 4).

Pressures of labor costs on prices were relieved by the surge in productivity growth, permitting unusually large increases in real earnings with a somewhat less rapid rise in wage rates than earlier. The large increases in output were accompanied by rising profits and

Table 4

AVERAGE HOURLY EARNINGS BEFORE AND AFTER ADJUSTMENTS FOR CONSUMER PRICE INCREASES AND OUTPUT PER MAN-HOUR, PRIVATE NONFARM AND MANUFACTURING SECTORS

(annual percentage change)

	Average for 1959–69	1969	1970	1971	1972	1973
Average hourly earnings, private nonfarm economy [a]						
Current dollars	4.1	6.6	6.7	7.0	6.3	6.2
Adjusted for consumer price changes	1.2	1.2	0.7	2.6	3.0	0.0
Output per man-hour, private nonfarm economy	2.6	−0.2	0.7	4.1	4.2	2.7
Average hourly earnings, manufacturing [a]						
Current dollars	3.7	6.0	6.2	6.6	6.2	5.8
Adjusted for consumer price changes	1.3	0.7	0.2	2.2	2.9	−0.4
Output per man-hour, manufacturing	3.2	2.6	0.6	6.8	6.4	5.9

[a] Average hourly earnings for production and nonsupervisory workers adjusted for overtime (in manufacturing only) and interindustry employment shifts. The consumer price index was used to adjust for consumer price changes.

Source: U.S. Department of Labor, Bureau of Labor Statistics.

Table 5

PROFITS AND INCOME SHARES FOR THE CORPORATE SECTOR AND NONFINANCIAL CORPORATIONS

	Average for 1959–69	1969	1970	1971	1972	1973
All corporations						
Profits ($ billions) [a]	65.0	75.3	64.5	73.8	86.9	97.8
Percentage change in profits	2.5	−6.2	−14.3	14.4	17.8	12.5
Profits share [b]	17.4	14.2	11.8	12.6	13.4	13.6
Compensation share [b]	64.9	66.4	67.4	66.5	66.4	66.9
Nonfinancial corporations						
Profits ($ billions) [a]	54.8	62.9	50.9	58.3	69.3	78.2
Percentage change in profits	3.9	−8.8	−19.1	14.6	18.9	12.8
Profits share [b]	15.2	12.5	9.8	10.5	11.3	11.4
Compensation share [b]	64.2	65.7	66.9	66.0	65.9	66.4

[a] Profits and inventory valuation adjustment.

[b] Share of gross product originating in sector.

Source: U.S. Department of Commerce, Social and Economic Statistics Administration, Bureau of Economic Analysis.

some rise in the profits share, although the employee compensation share remained unusually high during the cyclical expansion (Table 5). These conditions during 1972 help to account for the degree of public acceptance of controls at that time and for the underlying cooperation of organized labor evidenced by the low incidence of work stoppages.

In 1973 price increases accelerated sharply, at the outset mostly for food, and the acceleration in inflation at the consumer level was heavily concentrated in food throughout most of the year. A continuation of relatively moderate wage increases led to a decline in real earnings, even though labor costs per unit of output rose more rapidly when productivity increases tapered off during 1973. Most of the acceleration in price increases, however, can be traced to factors other than larger increases in unit labor costs.

The price surge of 1973 was dominated by developments that were largely outside of the aggregative domestic cost and price relationships that have received most attention in formulating projections of price performance. The main exogenous elements were the decline in world food supply, the further devaluation and subsequent slide in the value of the dollar, the strength and coincidence of the boom in most large industrial countries, and by fall, the oil embargo and action taken by the international cartel to raise prices. In addition, a number of basic materials industries were operating at capacity production levels, though this was belatedly recognized (Table 6). While the inflation was supported by a period of rapid monetary expansion, these developments through their influence on domestic supply and prices had a major impact on short-term inflation. It is possible, however, that delays in price increases induced by the controls contributed to the persistence of overly expansionary policies by delaying the recognition of inflationary pressures in 1972 and early 1973.

Wages

Wage increases, as measured by adjusted average hourly earnings, were somewhat smaller in percentage terms in 1972 and 1973 than in the preceding four years. The decline in new first-year wage increases under major collective bargaining agreements was much more pronounced. In manufacturing, for example, the average increase declined from 10.9 percent in 1971 to 6.6 percent in 1972. The decline in construction wage increases began in 1971, coincident with the introduction of controls, and new first-year increases declined from an average of 17.6 percent in 1970 to 5.0 percent in 1973. While this shows that wages increased less rapidly under the controls than before the controls, the extent to which the slowdown was attributable to the controls is not clear.

Wage structural developments in the period immediately before institution of controls had created conditions favorable for achieving smaller wage increases by 1972. Deferred wage increases scheduled for 1972 were somewhat lower on average than those for 1971, and most workers with contracts expiring in 1972 had received relatively large increases during the term of their contracts. Their position in the wage structure compared to relative positions of other unionized workers had not deteriorated significantly. Moreover, workers in nonunion manufacturing establishments received smaller wage increases in 1970 and 1971 than those in union establishments. Thus

Table 6

CAPACITY UTILIZATION RATES

(seasonally adjusted)

		Major Materials Industries						
	Manufacturing	Total	Durable goods	Nondurable goods	Metals	Textiles	Paper and pulp	Chemicals and petroleum
1959–69 average		85.5	80.0	88.0	79.9	87.8	91.1	86.6
1969	86.5	90.0	87.6	90.9	89.4	87.8	95.5	90.1
1970	78.3	86.2	83.6	87.2	85.1	82.1	91.4	86.3
1971	75.0	85.3	78.8	87.6	76.1	84.3	92.5	86.6
1972	78.6	89.6	84.7	91.3	82.7	89.0	96.9	90.3
1973	83.0	93.3	91.8	93.9	91.7	94.5	96.5	93.0
1971 I	74.8	86.4	85.5	86.8	85.9	82.6	91.8	85.4
II	75.6	87.3	85.7	87.8	85.3	84.9	91.6	87.0
III	74.7	83.2	69.8	88.1	64.0	85.1	93.0	87.1
IV	74.6	84.3	74.0	88.0	69.0	84.7	93.7	86.7
1972 I	75.4	87.1	80.3	89.5	76.0	86.1	96.2	88.2
II	77.6	88.7	82.3	90.9	79.8	89.2	96.6	90.0
III	79.4	90.6	86.9	91.8	85.6	88.8	97.1	91.1
IV	81.5	92.1	89.1	93.1	89.3	91.9	97.5	92.0
1973 I	82.8	92.8	90.0	93.7	88.0	94.6	96.1	92.9
II	83.3	92.8	88.8	94.2	87.4	94.6	95.6	93.9
III	83.3	94.3	94.0	94.4	94.9	94.6	98.0	93.3
IV	82.6	93.4	94.3	93.2	96.4	94.3	96.4	91.9
1974 I	80.5	90.2	90.3	90.2	91.3	92.5	95.1	87.2
II	80.1	90.0	89.5	90.2	90.7	90.2	96.6	87.8

Source: Federal Reserve Board of Governors.

the wages of most workers with wage agreements scheduled to expire in 1972 were in better balance with wages of other workers in the economy than had been the wages of those covered by contracts expiring in 1970 or 1971. Moreover, the shift from acceleration to a slight deceleration in consumer price increases meant that an improved balance between wage increases and price increases had emerged after the catch-up process that occurred in the late 1960s.

Wage structural conditions in 1972 also pointed to the prospect of moderate settlements in 1973. The collective bargaining calendar was dominated by a few large contract situations, and the available evidence indicated that wages under most of the largest contracts expiring in 1973 had increased during the term of these contracts at least as rapidly as had the wages of the average worker. This pattern is illustrated for three major sectors in Table 7. The lack of evidence of deterioration in the relative wage positions of workers under contracts expiring in 1973 is in striking contrast to the pattern in the late 1960s (see Table 1). Moreover, the slower price increases of 1972 permitted unusually large real wage gains for most workers, including those with contracts expiring in 1973.

The wage situation in construction and in some other sectors was more complex. First-year wage increases in construction, after accelerating throughout the late 1960s, reached an average rate of increase above 17 percent in 1970, and normal wage patterns within the industry were severely disrupted. The extremely large wage increases in construction were considered by many observers to be creating wage structural pressures in other sectors, as workers with comparable skills sought comparable wage increases. The disorderly

Table 7

AVERAGE HOURLY EARNINGS CHANGES, SELECTED INDUSTRIES WITH A HIGH PROPORTION OF WORKERS COVERED BY LONG-TERM CONTRACTS EXPIRING IN 1973

	Increase in Average Hourly Earnings (percent)	
Industry Sector	1971	1972
Private nonfarm	6.5	6.4
Rubber	6.5	7.6
Autos	12.3	8.1
Trucking	13.3	10.8

Source: U.S. Department of Labor, Bureau of Labor Statistics.

wage structural conditions that emerged, both within the construction sector and for wages of workers in other sectors with skills similar to those of construction workers, do not lend themselves to a simple interpretation. They represented developments more complex than simple restoration of a balance in relative wages that had been disrupted primarily through inflation. Consequently, there is no strong basis for confidence that the pattern of leapfrogging and catch-up would have been broken in the absence of controls. The timing and magnitude of the decline in new wage increases in construction in 1971 and 1972 provide strong circumstantial evidence that a significant influence should be attributed to the controls in that sector.[3] Moreover, smaller wage increases in construction under wage controls may have contributed indirectly to wage stabilization in other sectors. Since construction wage levels were already relatively high, it would have been extremely difficult to achieve smaller wage increases in other sectors and a restoration of more normal wage structural patterns in the absence of a sharp reduction in construction wage increases.

For most sectors the fact that new wage increases under collective bargaining agreements in 1972 and 1973 were smaller than those in 1970 and 1971 fits the pattern expected on the basis of wage structural developments. Much of the decline in wage increases could have been the result of factors other than the controls, although controls may have facilitated a more rapid realization of smaller wage increases. Wage structural developments undoubtedly contributed to the acquiescence of organized labor in settlements with smaller wage increases in 1972 and 1973 than had been obtained in other settlements. The fact that the Pay Board approved higher wage increases in the union than in the nonunion sector, the concentration of wage cutbacks in the union sector, a declining differential between wage increases for union and nonunion workers in manufacturing in 1972, and the reduced dispersion in the size of new wage settlements in 1972 and 1973 are all consistent with the view that an important role should be attributed to changing wage structural conditions.

Assessment of the contribution of controls to the reduction in the size of new wage increases under collective bargaining agreements in 1972 and 1973 is complicated by the influence of wage structural

[3] An estimate of the impact on construction wage increases of the Construction Industry Stabilization Committee was developed by D. Q. Mills in "Explaining Pay Increases in Construction: 1953-1972," *Industrial Relations*, May 1974, pp. 196-201. His estimate of a 2.5 percent annual effect in reducing construction wage increases is, as he notes, sensitive to the treatment of the significant influence of a wage structure variable incorporated into his analysis.

changes. In Table 8, data on the distribution of wage increases under major agreements show a pronounced reduction in the proportion of wage increases that exceeded 8 and 10 percent in 1972 and 1973. Although changes in wage structural conditions provided grounds for expecting fewer very large wage increases after 1971, wage controls may have helped to ensure that restoration of wage structural balance was accompanied by a reduction in average wage increases.

It has often been suggested that setting a standard or guideline as a ceiling for wage increases also tends to set a floor.[4] The evidence from the data in Table 8 is mixed. A larger proportion of settlements with wage increases below 5 and 6 percent occurred during the two years of controls than during the preceding two years. However, by 1973 wage increases were also far more heavily concentrated in the 5 to 6 percent range than they had been previously. Since the wage standard was implemented for a period too short to assure that its full consequences had become evident, and since little confidence can be placed in projections of the proportion of small wage increases that was most likely in the absence of controls, these data provide at best only weak evidence on this issue.

Another issue that has undergone considerable debate is the effectiveness of a simple numerical guideline or standard for wage stabilization. The standards and computational procedures established during Phase II were neither strongly reaffirmed nor explicitly disavowed in 1973; they were, however, used along with other criteria under an approach in which the idea of a single standard applicable to all wage situations was explicitly rejected. These data indicate, however, that the dispersion in actual wage settlements was smaller in 1973 and average increases were smaller, both for all industries and within manufacturing, than in 1972. The standards were apparently administered more flexibly in 1972 than was generally recognized, and they resulted in lower average increases in 1973 than in 1972, in spite of the announced intentions to administer them with more flexibility.

Prices

The goal of a 2 to 3 percent rate of inflation by the end of 1972 was established when controls were introduced. This represented a con-

[4] This argument is noted, for example, in Robert M. Solow, "The Case against the Case against the Guideposts," in *Guidelines, Informal Controls and the Marketplace*, ed. George P. Shultz and Robert Z. Aliber (Chicago: University of Chicago Press, 1966), p. 45, and in a *New York Times* article of 1 March 1973 by Edward Cowan, entitled "U.S. Aide Outlines Tactics on Wages."

Table 8

FIRST-YEAR WAGE RATE CHANGES IN COLLECTIVE BARGAINING AGREEMENTS COVERING 1,000 WORKERS OR MORE

	Percentage of Workers Affected							
	All industries				Manufacturing			
Type of Wage Rate Action	1970	1971	1972	1973	1970	1971	1972	1973
No wage increase	—	1	3	1	—	1	2	—
Increase in wages	100	99	98	99	100	99	98	100
Less than 4 percent	1	1	8	8	1	2	4	4
4 to 5 percent	1	1	6	17	1	2	7	5
5 to 6 percent	3	3	20	30	6	4	23	47
6 to 7 percent	17	9	21	22	33	16	26	24
7 to 8 percent	11	5	14	9	18	7	20	7
8 to 10 percent	13	17	15	10	16	15	14	12
More than 10 percent	54	61	13	3	24	53	5	—
Not specified	1	1	—	—	—	—	—	—
Total wage actions	100	100	100	100	100	100	100	100
Number of workers (000)	4,675	3,978	2,424	5,320	2,184	1,913	913	2,318
Mean adjustment (percent)	11.9	11.6	7.3	5.8	8.1	10.9	6.6	5.9
Median adjustment (percent)	10.0	12.5	6.6	5.5	7.5	10.1	6.2	5.5

Source: U.S. Department of Labor, Bureau of Labor Statistics.

siderable reduction from the 6 percent increase in consumer prices during 1969. However, the upper range of the goal was a modest target compared to the 3.6 percent rate of increase during the first eight months of 1971. The belief that the goal was within reach was bolstered by the fact that consumer prices were increasing at about a 3 percent rate in mid–1972. More rapid increases in food prices in late 1972, reflected most strongly in the wholesale price index, pointed toward a temporary acceleration in consumer price inflation. But since the acceleration was mainly limited to the farm and food sector, the acceleration in inflation from this source could be reversed relatively quickly by appropriately expansionary farm policies if crop conditions were favorable.

This prospect was shattered by the size and persistence of the farm and food price increases, along with the unexpected emergence of tight markets and sharp price increases in several other critical sectors. Thus the initial promise of progress toward renewed price stability, nurtured in part by the initial apparent success of Phase II, was followed by a surge in inflation to almost unprecedented rates in spite of efforts to restructure the controls to contain it.

Evaluation of the influence of controls on prices is facilitated by examining the sectoral incidence of inflation and of its acceleration during the period. The pass-through of increased costs formed the basis for price adjustments, and in several sectors prices of inputs that accounted for a major share of total costs were exempt from controls. As a result, control in these sectors was exerted only on processing and distribution markups, and prices in these sectors could rise dramatically under the stabilization rules in contrast to other sectors in which most of the major inputs were domestically produced and subject to controls. Moreover, increases in prices of major inputs and pass-through of these increased input costs to higher product prices were generally permitted when demand conditions in the marketplace supported them. This approach was necessary in view of the limited supplementary role intended for controls and the reluctance to take complementary measures such as subsidies, rationing, or export controls that would have been necessary if a more ambitious role had been assigned to controls.

During 1972, disproportionate contributions to inflation came from the food component of the consumer price index and the farm products and processed food and feeds component of the wholesale price index (Table 9). Increases in wholesale industrial prices were disproportionately concentrated in lumber and hides. In all of these sectors, major inputs were exempt from controls. Demand pressures

Table 9

CONSUMER PRICES AND WHOLESALE PRICES BY PHASES OF THE STABILIZATION PROGRAM: PERCENT CHANGES FOR SELECTED COMPONENTS

(seasonally adjusted compound annual rates)

Price Indexes and Components	1969 12 Months (12/68–12/69) [a]	1970 12 Months (12/69–12/70) [a]	1971 8 Months Prior to Freeze (12/70–8/71)	Phase I 3 Months (8/71–11/71)	Phase II 14 Months (11/71–1/73)	Phase III 5 Months (1/73–6/73)	Freeze II 2 Months (6/73–8/73)	Phase IV 8 Months (8/73–4/74)	Post-Controls 8 Months (4/74–12/74)
CONSUMER PRICE INDEX									
All items	6.1	5.5	3.6	2.0	3.7	8.3	3.8 [c]	11.5 [c]	12.2
Food	7.2	·2.2	4.7	1.3	6.7	20.8	0.9 [c]	17.9 [c]	11.7
Meat, poultry, and fish	11.2	–.6	2.2	6.6	13.0	39.6	–13.5 [c]	5.9 [c]	3.6
Nonfood commodities	4.5	4.8	2.6	1.0	2.5	4.6	3.0	11.1	12.6
Energy products [b]	3.1	3.6	0.7	–.7	2.4	18.3	2.5	62.1	3.9
Services [a]	7.4	8.2	4.5	3.1	3.5	4.3	5.3	9.5	12.5
All items except food	5.7	6.5	3.4	2.3	2.8	5.0	3.7	10.4	12.2
WHOLESALE PRICE INDEX									
All commodities	4.8	2.2	4.5	2.0	6.8	21.7	–13.7 [c]	19.7 [c]	19.8
Farm products and processed foods and feeds	7.5	–1.4	5.5	6.5	14.9	50.2	–34.0 [c]	13.6 [c]	13.8
Farm products	8.4	–4.7	7.0	6.9	20.7	75.5	–35.0 [c]	12.4 [c]	–1.4
Processed foods and feeds	6.8	0.8	4.6	5.0	11.4	38.2	–34.9 [c]	14.8 [c]	25.9
Industrial commodities	3.9	3.6	3.9	1.1	3.6	10.8	4.8	24.0	22.5
Hides	3.7	.5	4.6	3.2	21.0	–6.0	11.6	1.2	0.2
Fuels	4.0	11.1	–.1	2.5	5.9	19.1	10.4	76.3	51.9

Lumber	−8.3	−4.4	29.6	2.4	12.0	46.4	−9.6	14.0	−17.7
Metals	9.8	2.7	6.1	1.0	3.3	10.8	9.5	31.4	25.2
Selected stage of processing indexes									
Crude materials except food	10.6	4.7	2.1	2.6	10.8	23.9	18.2	69.1	1.1
Intermediate materials except food	3.8	3.2	5.8	1.0	4.0	12.9	4.8	25.8	25.4
Consumer goods except food	2.9	3.9	1.9	1.1	2.4	7.0	3.6	18.6	17.8

a Not seasonally adjusted.

b Index is calculated as a weighted average of the indexes for gasoline, motor oil, fuel oil, and coal, using December 1972 weights.

c For these components price changes are measured using July 1973 instead of August 1973 to reflect the early release from the sixty-day freeze of food prices on 18 July 1973.

Source: U.S. Department of Labor, Bureau of Labor Statistics.

were transmitted throughout the processing and distribution chain, a process that kept cost increases, except for costs of producing exempt products, roughly consistent with product price increases. In the first three quarters of 1973, food prices rose rapidly, and rapid increases in exempt farm product prices accounted for much of their acceleration. In the last part of the year, the contribution of petroleum and energy prices to inflation was extraordinarily large, despite the fact that petroleum and other energy products represented only small components of the indexes. In both sectors, increased costs were quickly reflected in higher consumer prices because the time spent in the production and distribution chain is relatively short. While the prices of both farm products and petroleum products were strongly influenced by developments in international markets, pressure on domestic prices came from export demand in the case of farm products and from rising import prices in the case of petroleum products.

The strength of demand in both domestic and foreign markets and the devaluation of the dollar combined to support higher prices for a widening range of basic materials. These higher prices were initially reflected primarily in the wholesale price index. In 1973 prices of basic materials and partially processed materials, which constituted 30 percent of the industrial component of wholesale prices, accounted for about 75 percent of the overall increase in industrial prices. These increased costs for processors and distributors were reflected in the latter part of 1973 and in 1974 by price increases for other commodities in the wholesale price index and higher consumer prices.

There was considerable scope for price increases within the limits of the stabilization rules at the beginning of 1973. The extent to which the prices of commodities in the industrial component of the wholesale price index could rise during 1972 and early 1973 before reaching levels authorized from the outset of the freeze in August 1971 is shown in Table 10. Much of the room for price increases was concentrated in the three sectors shown separately, and the amount of room left was rapidly shrinking in the first part of 1973. The tabulation does not take into account, however, the additional authority for price increases granted by the Price Commission during Phase II. Many companies in each of these sectors, and most of the major companies in the chemical industry, were authorized under term limit pricing agreements to raise prices by an average of

Table 10

WHOLESALE PRICES OF INDUSTRIAL PRODUCTS BELOW INITIAL PRICE CEILINGS: NUMBER OF ITEMS AND PERCENTAGE IMPACT FOR SELECTED MONTHS, DECEMBER 1971 THROUGH APRIL 1973

Industrial Commodities below Apparent Price Ceilings	December 1971	June 1972	December 1972	April 1973
Wholesale industrial commodities (73.162)[a]				
Number of commodities below ceilings	553	496	473	366
Impact of rise to ceilings	1.82	1.54	1.46	.90
Chemicals and allied products (5.716)				
Number	69	78	78	69
Impact	.22	.21	.21	.17
Metals and metal products (13.439)				
Number	127	113	109	68
Impact	.74	.65	.62	.25
Machinery and equipment (12.280)				
Number	138	142	141	120
Impact	.32	.34	.34	.26
All other components (41.627)				
Number	219	163	145	109
Impact	.54	.34	.29	.22

Note: Apparent initial price ceilings are defined as the highest prices of four months: May 1970, June 1970, July 1971, and August 1971. Prices in these months were chosen to approximate the alternate price ceilings of 25 May 1970 in the legislation and those of the base period for the freeze in the thirty days prior to 15 August 1971. Measures of the impact of a rise in prices to apparent initial ceiling levels are estimates of the percentage impact on the industrial commodities component of the wholesale price index.

a Numbers in parentheses reflect relative importance in December 1971.

Source: U.S. Department Labor, Bureau of Labor Statistics.

1.8 to 2 percent above the stated levels.[5] By November 1972, after submission of prenotification requests, price increases averaging between 3 and 4 percent had been approved covering a large proportion of the sales of large firms in each of these sectors. Much of the

5 For an analysis of term limit pricing agreements, see Frederic L. Laughlin, "An Evaluation of the Price Commission's Policy of Term Limit Pricing during Phase II of the Economic Stabilization Program" (Ph.D. diss., The George Washington University, 1975).

acceleration in wholesale price increases in early 1973 represented increases toward previously authorized levels.

To assess the extent to which price increases during the program were consistent with the cost pass-through rules, cost and price trends that occurred can be compared. Because labor costs constitute a major share of value added, it is instructive to compare unit labor cost increases and implicit price deflator increases for the private nonfarm and nonfinancial corporate sectors during the period of controls. There was an unusually close correspondence between price and unit labor cost increases during 1972, and price increases were smaller than unit labor cost increases in 1973.[6] The close correspondence during 1972 and early 1973 is particularly striking in view of the typical cyclical pattern, at least prior to 1968, of price increases exceeding unit labor cost increases when demand and output increases were large. To adjust for this cyclical influence, predicted differences for the period beginning with the last quarter of 1971 were developed on the basis of a regression fitted to the preceding period including real output changes and the unemployment rate.[7] The predicted differences are compared with actual differences in Figures 4 and 5, and the charts show substantially smaller price increases relative to unit labor cost increases than predicted throughout the period of controls. Those data strongly suggest that price increases conformed more closely to unit labor cost increases under the cost pass-through

[6] Figures A-1 and A-2 in the Appendix show quarterly percentage changes from the preceding year in implicit prices, unit labor costs, and their differences for the private nonfarm and nonfinancial corporate sectors. Means and standard deviations for the difference between year-to-year changes in prices and unit labor costs were as follows:

		Private nonfarm		*Nonfinancial corporations*
Mean	(1950-73)	−0.11	(1959-73)	−0.06
Standard deviation	(1950-73)	2.47	(1959-73)	2.45
Standard deviation	(1971/IV-1973/IV)	.69	(1971/IV-1973/IV)	.82

[7] The basic data for the regressions are:

	Constant term	*Percent change in real output*	*Unemployment rate*	*Standard error of estimate*
Private nonfarm sector (90 observations) $R^2 = .57$	−5.4	.28 S.E. = (.03)	.89 S.E. = (.10)	1.08
Nonfinancial corporations (51 observations) $R^2 = .74$	−6.5	.30 S.E. = (.03)	1.01 S.E. = (.12)	.88

Serial correlation was high with a Durbin-Watson statistic of .5 for each regression.

Figure 4

CHANGES IN PRICES AND UNIT LABOR COSTS FOR NONFINANCIAL CORPORATIONS, PREDICTED AND ACTUAL, 1959–73

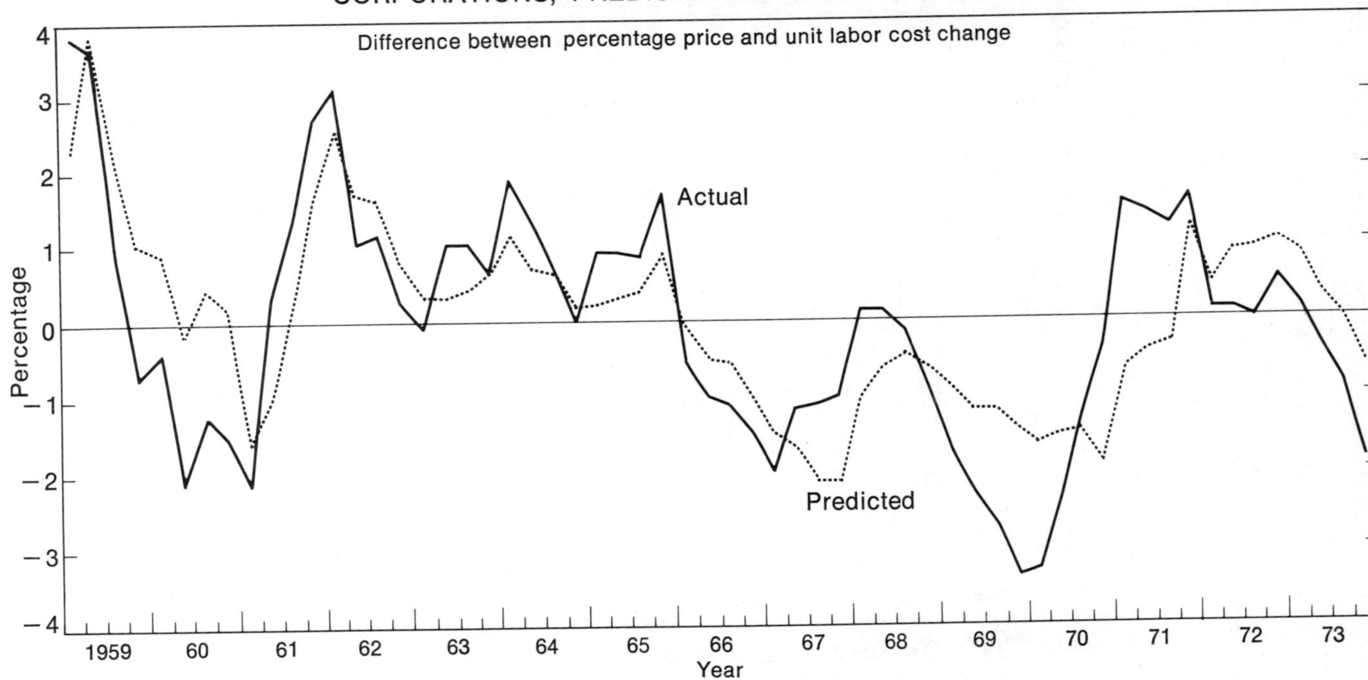

Note: Quarterly percentage change in prices minus percentage change in unit labor costs measured from four quarters earlier.
Source: Bureau of Labor Statistics.

Figure 5

CHANGES IN PRICES AND UNIT LABOR COSTS IN THE PRIVATE NONFARM SECTOR, PREDICTED AND ACTUAL, 1950–73

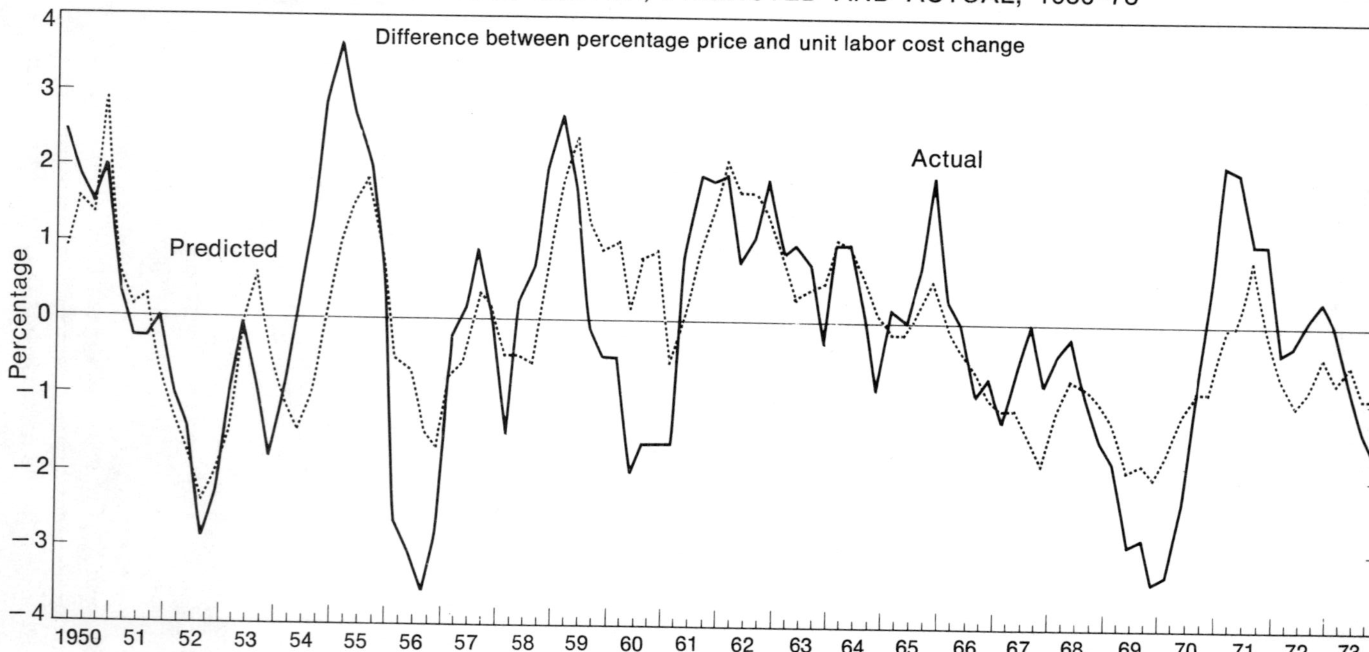

Note: Quarterly percentage change in prices minus percentage change in unit labor costs measured from four quarters earlier.
Source: Bureau of Labor Statistics.

rules of the controls than would have been expected at that stage of the cycle without the cost pass-through rules.

Profits

Corporate profits rose by an average of 15 percent per year from 1970 to 1973, after declining by an average of 12 percent per year from 1968 to 1970. The pretax corporate profits share rose from 11.8 percent in 1970 to 13.4 percent in 1972 and 13.6 percent in 1973, but remained well below its average level of 17.4 percent during the 1960s. Profits are highly cyclical, and it is difficult to compare their actual performance in 1971–73 with performance that would normally be expected in a cyclical recovery. It is instructive, however, to analyze the extent to which profit trends during this period were consistent with the stabilization rules and to examine the relationship between price and profit margin changes.

In the simplest analytic framework, the cost pass-through rules for price adjustments suggest that percentage profit margins on sales should remain constant with percentage cost pass-through and decline with dollar-for-dollar pass-through of costs. This analytic framework, however, does not take into account possibilities for input substitution, short-term productivity changes that differ from those applied during the program, changes in product mix, and the effect of increased volume on fixed costs per unit of output. Thus actual profit margins could rise within the framework of the stabilization regulations.

The consistency of profit performance with the stabilization regulations is explored in Tables 11 through 13 along with the influence of alternative pricing rules and short-term productivity changes on profits and prices. The analysis is focused mainly on profits, value added, and implicit price deflators for the nonfinancial corporate sector, because the coverage and the procedural requirements of the controls were concentrated on large firms and these data are readily available. These data permit some judgments on the behavior of costs, prices, and profits in relation to the regulations. The period over which the analysis is made begins with the first quarter of 1971, because price increases under the stabilization regulations could be linked to cost increases that occurred no earlier than the beginning of 1971.

The predominant share of the increase in profits during the entire period from the first quarter of 1971 to the second quarter of 1974 can be attributed to the increase in the current dollar value of output

Table 11

PROFITS AND PROFIT MARGINS FOR NONFINANCIAL CORPORATIONS: QUARTERLY AND CUMULATIVE CHANGES FROM 1971–I THROUGH 1974–II

	Actual Changes in Profits (1)	Calculated Changes in Profits: Maintenance of constant percentage margin (2)	Departure from constant percentage margin (3)	Difference between constant percentage and constant dollar margin[a] (4)
Quarterly Periods	Quarterly Profits Changes ($ billions, annual rates)			
1971 II	2.6	1.1	1.5	0.5
III	1.2	0.8	0.4	0.3
IV	0.5	1.2	−0.7	0.1
1972 I	5.1	2.3	2.8	0.6
II	2.3	1.8	0.5	0.2
III	2.3	1.2	1.1	0.2
IV	5.7	2.4	3.3	0.5
1973 I	2.9	2.8	0.1	0.6
II	0.4	1.8	−1.4	0.9
III	−0.5	1.3	−1.8	0.9
IV	−0.2	1.7	−1.9	1.4
1974 I	−4.1	0.5	−4.6	2.1
II	3.2	1.9	1.3	2.2
Cumulative Periods	Cumulative Profits Changes[b] ($ billions)			
1971 IV	1.1	0.8	0.3	0.2
1972 IV	4.9	2.7	2.3	0.6
1973 IV	5.6	4.6	1.0	1.5
1974 II	5.4	5.2	0.2	2.6

Note: Profits are measured before taxes and include the inventory valuation adjustment, and output is measured in terms of value added as reported in the national income accounts.

[a] This increment to profits is calculated as the difference between the increase in profits that would maintain constant percentage profit margins and the increase that would be sufficient only to keep profits per unit of real output constant. It represents the amount by which profits would need to be augmented to compensate for inflation in order to avoid a reduction in the profits share.

[b] Cumulative profits changes are smaller than the sum of quarterly changes by approximately a factor of 4 because quarterly changes are expressed at annual rates, and quarterly changes may not sum to totals of 4 times cumulative changes because of rounding. Cumulative totals for components may differ in addition because they were calculated on the basis of the percentage margin prevailing in the first quarter of 1971.

Source: Computed from data from U.S. Department of Commerce, Bureau of Economic Analysis.

during that period rather than to a rise in percentage profit margins. Of the $5.4 billion cumulative increase in profits for nonfinancial corporations during the second quarter of 1974 (column 1, Table 11), $5.2 billion was required to maintain a constant percentage profit margin (column 2, Table 11). About half of this component of profits reflected rising prices (column 4, Table 11) with the other half reflecting increased real output. Only a tiny fraction of the increase in profits in this quarter was accounted for by an increase in percentage profit margins (column 3, Table 11). Also, by the second quarter of 1974 the profits share of gross product originating in nonfinancial corporations was only 10.5 percent compared to an average of 15.2 percent during the 1960s.

There was a great deal of variation in overall changes in profits during the period, however, and in the extent to which such changes in profits reflected changes in percentage profit margins. By the end of 1972, wider percentage profit margins accounted for nearly as much of the cumulative increase in profits as the increased value of output at constant percentage margins. On the other hand, by the second quarter of 1974 wider margins accounted for only a minute share of the cumulative increase in profits (columns 2 and 3, Table 11). The extent to which profits increases consistent with maintaining constant percentage margins reflected rising real output or rising prices also shifted markedly during the period. The calculated increment to profits resulting from the difference between constant percentage and constant dollar profit margins was very small through 1972 ($.6 billion out of $2.7 billion), but it increased sharply when prices were rising more rapidly during 1973 and early 1974. By the second quarter of 1974 half of the profits increase associated with maintaining constant percentage margins was accounted for by higher prices instead of by increased real output.

The difference between constant percentage and constant dollar profit margins per unit of real output corresponds closely in concept to the difference between price adjustments to reflect percentage pass-through or price adjustments to reflect dollar-for-dollar pass-through of increased costs. Because these calculations (column 4, Table 11) are based on value-added measures of real output, the calculated difference in profits understates the impact on profits of the difference in cost pass-through concepts. The impact of the difference between percentage and dollar-for-dollar cost pass-through may be understated by approximately a factor of two when the costs of materials inputs are rising at about the same rate as costs of the value-added component of prices.

The applicability of these aggregative comparisons of percentage and dollar-for-dollar cost pass-through is also limited by the fact that the cost pass-through regulations were applied in different ways for particular sectors. For example, the retail and wholesale sectors were permitted to apply percentage markups to the cost of merchandise throughout this period as well as in earlier stabilization programs. In certain sectors, such as meat packing, where prices of major inputs were highly volatile, price adjustments were permitted during the entire period only to reflect dollar-for-dollar pass-through of major input costs. It is difficult to be precise about the quantitative influence of constant percentage or constant dollar profit margins, but it is worth noting that the impact of the difference between percentage and dollar-for-dollar cost pass-through is disproportionately large for profit margins compared to its implications for price changes. The increment to profits necessary to maintain constant percentage profit margins, by reflecting the rise in prices at a given output level, accounted for about 50 percent of the increase in profits over the entire period but only 1.5 percentage points of the 15 percent rise in prices (columns 1 and 4, Table 13).

Short-term changes in output per man-hour resulted in changes in the relationship between revenues and costs that could be reflected in changes in profit margins within the framework of the stabilization regulations. This source of short-term variation in profit margins was of most importance during the stabilization program, and it is also more readily susceptible to quantification than other possible sources such as changes in product mix or input substitution. In reviewing requests for price increases, short-term production and sales volume changes were taken into account to some extent, but their influence was small and difficult to estimate in the absence of information on actual and expected sales volumes. Under the stabilization regulations, net increases in labor costs were calculated on the basis of trend rates of increase in output per man-hour. The difference between short-term output per man-hour changes and these trend rates was used to calculate the potential influence on profits from this source. The results are shown in Table 12 along with actual changes in profit margins. This source more than accounts for the actual widening of profit margins for nonfinancial corporations through 1972, and it accounts for about half of the smaller cumulative rise in profit margins through 1973 (columns 3 and 4, Table 12). After the first quarter of 1973, percentage profit margins declined as output per man-hour increases fell far below trend rates.

Table 12

OUTPUT PER MAN-HOUR CHANGES AND PROFIT MARGINS FOR NONFINANCIAL CORPORATIONS: QUARTERLY AND CUMULATIVE CHANGES FROM 1971–I THROUGH 1974–II

	Percentage Change in Output per Man-Hour (1)	**Difference between Trend Rate and Short-Term Output per Man-Hour Change**[a] (2)	**Difference in Rates of Output per Man-Hour Change**[b] (3)	**Change in Percentage Profit Margin**[c] (4)
Quarterly Periods	Quarterly Output per Man-Hour Measures		Quarterly Calculated Increments to Profits ($ billions, annual rates)	
1971 II	0.9	0.1	0.3	1.5
III	1.6	0.8	2.9	0.4
IV	0.7	−0.1	−0.4	−0.7
1972 I	1.8	1.0	3.8	2.8
II	1.0	0.2	0.9	0.5
III	1.1	0.3	1.2	1.1
IV	1.1	0.3	1.2	3.3
1973 I	2.0	1.2	5.0	0.1
II	0.2	−0.6	−2.8	−1.4
III	0.2	−0.6	−2.9	−1.8
IV	−0.6	−1.5	−6.7	−1.9
1974 I	−1.4	−2.2	−10.3	−4.6
II	0.3	−0.5	−2.3	1.3
Cumulative Periods[d]	Cumulative Output per Man-Hour Measures		Cumulative Calculated Increments to Profits[e] ($ billions)	
1971 IV	3.2	0.8	0.7	0.3
1972 IV	8.3	2.6	2.5	2.3
1973 IV	9.9	1.0	0.6	1.0
1974 II	8.9	−1.6	−2.5	0.2

[a] The trend rate of increase in output per man-hour was calculated as the compound quarterly rate of increase from 1958 through 1969, the period used by the Price Commission for developing rates of productivity growth to be applied in estimating net increases in labor costs. The trend rate for the nonfinancial corporate sector was a 0.8 quarterly rate or a 3.2 percent annual rate.

[b] Increments to profits attributed to the difference between short-term and trend rates of change in output per man-hour are calculated by applying the differential in output per man-hour changes to the compensation share of value added in the nonfinancial corporate sector.

[c] From column 3, Table 11.

[d] Quarterly changes may not sum to cumulative totals because of rounding.

[e] Cumulative increments to profits are smaller than the sum of quarterly changes by approximately a factor of 4 because quarterly changes are expressed in terms of annual rates for compensation and profits. Quarterly changes may not sum to totals of 4 times cumulative changes because cumulative increments to profits were computed on the basis of the percentage margin prevailing in the first quarter of 1971.

Source: Computed from data from U.S. Department of Commerce, Bureau of Economic Analysis, and Department of Labor, Bureau of Labor Statistics.

Changes in profit margins during the entire period seem to be mainly attributable to cyclical developments, including changes in output per man-hour, instead of to changes in the controls. The rise in profit margins from the fourth quarter of 1971 to the first quarter of 1972 may have been influenced by the transition to Phase II, since prices also rose sharply, but it could also be accounted for by the sharp rise in output per man-hour. Similarly, the decline in profit margins in the last half of 1973 might be partly attributable to the second freeze and dollar-for-dollar pass-through of costs in Phase IV, but the decline had begun in the second quarter and could have been expected to continue on the basis of larger increases in costs.

The data on profit margin changes do not support the view that prices increased more rapidly than costs during Phase III. The acceleration of inflation that began in 1973 was in fact accompanied by a sharp reduction in percentage profit margin expansion in the first quarter when material input cost increases began accelerating. Percentage profit margins declined after the first quarter of 1973 as prices, unit labor costs, and other costs rose more rapidly.

Profits data on an annual basis for selected industries (Appendix Tables A-3 through A-5) indicate that manufacturing accounted for a major portion of profits increases in 1972 and agriculture accounted for a major portion of profits increases in 1973. In each case much of the increase in profits could be attributed to wider profit margins. However, the component of profits attributable to wider profit margins in manufacturing over the entire period, $6.9 billion, was small compared to the amount accounted for by large short-term productivity increases, $12.4 billion (Table A-5). In addition, because of the large size of the manufacturing sector, the increase in prices that was accompanied by profit margin widening was small compared to the increase in prices that was accompanied by profit margin widening in agriculture. With prices of raw agricultural products exempt, almost 30 percentage points of the increase in the price deflator for agriculture was associated with wider margins on value added, mainly during 1973. These data also show a slight narrowing of percentage margins for retail and wholesale trade in 1972 and 1973 even though both sectors were formally under regulations permitting constant percentage markups over costs.[8]

The profit margin data show a broad pattern of conformity with the regulations during the period of the controls. It must be recog-

[8] It was pointed out by Joel Popkin in "Prices in 1972: An Analysis of Changes during Phase II," *Monthly Labor Review*, vol. 96, no. 2 (February 1973), pp. 16-23, that prices of finished goods seemed to have risen by more at the manufacturing level than at the retail level during 1972.

nized, of course, in using profits data to examine the consistency of cost and price increases that there are limitations resulting from the presence of long-term contracts, the existence of inventories, and possibilities for hedging in purchasing and pricing policies. The data clearly show the importance of the unusually rapid short-term productivity gains during the early part of the period in providing additional real income that was accrued in the form of a slowing of price increases and a rise in profit margins. They also show that the expansion in profit margins that occurred during 1972 was consistent with the stabilization regulations in force, and that the acceleration in inflation occurring in early 1973 during Phase III was not accompanied by the wider profit margins that would be expected if business firms were raising prices more rapidly than their costs were increasing.

The limited potential of controls as a tool to improve price performance by squeezing profit margins is illustrated by the data on prices in Table 13. Only a small fraction of the overall change in prices during the period can be directly accounted for by conversion of the components of profits changes into corresponding changes in the value of output and prices. A major reason for the insensitivity of prices to profit margin changes is the small fraction of the value of output accounted for by profits. Profits accounted for less than 10 percent of output of nonfinancial corporations in 1970. The shift in output per man-hour and profit margin trends in early 1973 reduced the portion of the increase in prices related to change in percentage profit margins, but the shift to more rapid inflation increased the influence on prices of maintenance of percentage margins. Expansion of percentage margins after the first quarter of 1971, when they were near a cyclical as well as a historical low, accounted for less than one percentage point of the 8.7 percent cumulative rise in prices by the end of 1973, and only 0.3 out of 15 percent by the second quarter of 1974. Maintenance of percentage margins, through a rise in profits per unit of real output sufficient to compensate for the rise in output prices, accounted for an additional percentage point by the end of 1973 and 1.5 percentage points by the second quarter of 1974. These data show that the consequences of limiting percentage profit margins to their cyclically low level at the beginning of 1971, or reducing percentage margins through erosion of the profits share in real terms, could both have significant effects on the rates of return on investment and on cash flow available for investment in production capacity—even though price inflation in the corporate nonfinancial sector would not have been significantly affected. Moreover, the proportionate effect on consumer prices of a squeeze on profits would have been

Table 13

PRICES AND THEIR RELATION TO PROFITS AND OUTPUT PER MAN-HOUR CHANGES FOR NONFINANCIAL CORPORATIONS: QUARTERLY AND CUMULATIVE INCREMENTS FROM 1971–I THROUGH 1974–II

	Change in Implicit Price Deflator (1)	Change in Percentage Profit Margin [a] (2)	Difference in Rates of Output per Man-Hour Change [b] (3)	Difference between Constant Percentage and Constant Dollar Profit Margin [c] (4)
Quarterly Percentage Changes		Quarterly Calculated Increments to Price Change		
1971 II	0.8	0.2	0.1	0.1
III	0.6	0.1	0.5	0.1
IV	0.1	−0.1	−0.1	0.0
1972 I	0.9	0.5	0.7	0.1
II	0.2	0.1	0.1	0.0
III	0.4	0.2	0.2	0.0
IV	0.6	0.5	0.2	0.1
1973 I	0.7	0.0	0.8	0.1
II	1.1	−0.2	−0.4	0.1
III	1.1	−0.3	−0.4	0.1
IV	1.8	−0.3	−1.0	0.2
1974 I	2.7	−0.7	−1.5	0.3
II	3.0	0.2	−0.3	0.3
Cumulative Percentage Change [d]		Cumulative Calculated Increments to Price Change		
1971 IV	1.4	0.2	0.5	0.2
1972 IV	3.7	1.5	1.7	0.4
1973 IV	8.7	0.8	·0.6	0.9
1974 II	15.0	0.3	−1.2	1.5

[a] Calculations based on column 3, Table 11.

[b] Calculations based on column 3, Table 12.

[c] Calculations based on column 4, Table 11.

[d] Quarterly changes may not sum to cumulative totals because of rounding and cumulative totals for columns 2 and 4 may differ in addition because they are cumulated on the basis of the percentage margin prevailing in the first quarter of 1971.

Source: Same as for Table 12.

much smaller than for prices in the corporate nonfinancial sector during the period 1971–74, because prices of farm products and imported commodities (which are largely external to the corporate nonfinancial sector) were responsible for much of the acceleration in inflation that occurred in 1973.

Profit Margin Limitations

Prices could be increased under the stabilization regulations only if an increase in allowable costs could be demonstrated. While cost increases were a necessary condition for price increases, they were not a sufficient condition since limitations on profit margins were imposed in some form throughout the program. Realized profit margins as a percentage of sales were limited to levels achieved during a base period. The limitation was applied to individual firms and computed for the consolidated accounts of the parent firm instead of separately by divisions, profit centers, or other accounting entities. Base period limits for Phase II were established by computing the average profit margin for the best two of the three fiscal years completed immediately before 15 August 1971, with the inclusion of more recently completed fiscal years permitted after Phase III began in 1973.

Profit margin positions when the stabilization program began and developments during the program can be illustrated in general terms by Federal Trade Commission data for manufacturing corporations (Table 14). These data show that profit margins in the third quarter of 1971, when the stabilization program began, were on average considerably below the apparent limits established by the base period. For example, profit margins for all manufacturing averaged 8.6 percent in 1968 and 1969 compared to 6.9 percent in the third quarter of 1971 and 7.0 percent for the year. Relative to base period limits profit margins were then apparently highest for food and kindred products and tobacco manufacturers, with considerable room for expansion toward base period limits in most other sectors.

During 1972 manufacturing profit margins rose from 7.1 to 7.7 percent, remaining on average well below base period limits. Sectors in which margins rose most markedly toward base period limits included printing and publishing, rubber and plastics products, and lumber. Profit margins exceeding base period limits were reported during 1972 mainly by firms specializing in lumber production, although this is not apparent in the aggregate data.

Table 14

RELATION OF PROFITS BEFORE TAXES TO SALES, ALL MANUFACTURING CORPORATIONS, BY INDUSTRY GROUP, 1968–74

Year or Quarter		All Manufacturing Corporations	Nondurable Goods: Total nondurable	Food and kindred products	Tobacco manufactures	Textile mill products	Paper and allied products	Printing and publishing	Chemicals and allied products	Industrial chemicals and synthetics	Drugs	Petroleum and coal products	Rubber and miscellaneous plastic products
1968		8.8	8.4	4.9	11.4	6.1	8.2	7.8	12.5	11.2	18.6	12.0	8.3
1969		8.4	7.9	4.9	10.7	5.7	8.1	9.0	12.1	10.7	18.5	11.7	7.0
1970		6.8	7.3	4.8	11.2	4.1	5.7	8.0	10.7	8.5	17.2	11.0	5.1
1971		7.0	7.2	4.9	11.5	4.6	4.3	7.9	10.8	8.5	17.0	9.5	6.6
1972		7.5	7.2	4.6	11.0	4.8	6.8	8.7	11.2	9.3	17.8	8.5	7.4
1973		8.2	8.2	4.8	11.6	5.3	9.4	8.7	12.3	11.7	18.6	11.1	7.2
1971	III	6.9	7.5	5.2	12.1	4.7	4.5	8.0	11.1	8.5	17.4	10.2	6.5
	IV	6.9	6.7	4.6	11.2	5.9	3.2	9.0	10.0	6.5	17.5	8.1	6.8
1972	I	7.1	6.9	4.4	11.0	4.6	5.4	6.3	11.6	9.6	19.0	8.3	7.3
	II	7.8	7.1	4.8	11.5	4.6	7.6	8.9	11.1	10.3	18.1	7.1	8.0
	III	7.2	7.3	4.7	11.0	4.8	6.5	9.1	11.5	9.0	19.1	8.7	6.9
	IV	7.7	7.5	4.6	10.5	5.0	7.5	10.2	10.9	8.5	16.9	9.7	7.3
1973	I	7.9	7.2	4.4	10.3	5.2	8.0	7.5	12.2	11.3	18.6	8.4	6.9
	II	8.7	7.9	4.7	10.6	6.0	10.4	8.3	12.3	12.6	17.5	9.6	8.2
	III	7.7	7.8	4.8	10.7	5.1	9.8	9.1	12.1	10.9	18.8	10.5	5.8
	IV	8.7	9.6	5.2	15.7	4.8	9.2	9.8	12.8	11.9	20.0	16.6	7.7
1974	I	8.9	10.6	4.5	15.2	5.8	10.9	7.3	14.5	14.1	21.0	16.6	7.9
	II	9.6	11.1	4.6	18.1	6.5	13.4	9.7	15.6	16.5	20.8	14.5	9.8
Base period limit[a]		8.6	8.2	4.9	11.3	5.9	8.2	8.5	12.3	11.0	18.6	11.8	7.6

[a] Estimated for each industry by computing the average percentage profit margin for the two years in which profit margins were highest from calendar years 1968 through 1970.

Table 14 (continued)

Year or Quarter	Total durable	Transportation equipment	Motor vehicles and equipment	Aircraft and parts	Electrical machinery, equipment, and supplies	Machinery (except electrical)	Fabricated metal products	Primary metal industries	Primary iron and steel industries	Primary nonferrous metal industries	Stone, clay, and glass products	Lumber	Instruments and related products	Miscellaneous manufacturing (including ordnance)
	Durable Goods													
1968	9.1	9.1	10.9	6.0	8.1	10.7	7.7	8.4	7.5	9.7	9.3	8.4	15.4	7.7
1969	8.6	7.8	10.1	5.7	7.6	10.8	7.2	8.5	7.0	10.4	8.7	7.9	15.1	7.2
1970	6.3	3.8	4.0	3.5	6.1	9.2	5.8	5.9	3.6	8.9	6.6	4.4	13.7	6.3
1971	6.9	7.1	8.7	3.2	6.4	8.3	5.7	4.3	4.1	4.7	7.7	7.1	13.3	5.9
1972	7.7	7.6	9.1	4.4	7.2	9.3	6.5	5.2	5.0	5.6	8.0	8.0	14.5	6.3
1973	8.3	7.3	8.6	4.9	7.9	10.4	7.4	7.3	6.8	8.0	8.3	10.0	15.4	6.3
1971 III	6.3	4.7	4.8	4.0	6.6	8.0	6.3	0.8	0.2	1.7	9.3	7.9	14.7	7.1
IV	7.0	7.7	9.8	2.6	6.7	8.8	4.5	3.1	3.0	3.4	6.9	6.7	13.6	4.6
1972 I	7.3	8.3	10.4	3.9	6.4	8.8	5.9	4.6	4.0	5.7	5.6	7.0	13.0	5.2
II	8.6	9.4	11.2	5.1	7.1	9.7	7.2	6.2	5.9	6.8	9.6	9.1	14.9	6.7
III	7.1	4.1	4.0	4.3	7.1	9.5	6.9	4.2	4.0	4.6	9.5	9.1	15.5	6.3
IV	7.8	8.0	9.7	4.2	8.0	9.1	6.0	5.7	5.9	5.3	7.0	6.7	14.5	6.9
1973 I	8.5	9.5	11.3	4.9	7.6	10.0	6.9	6.2	5.9	6.8	6.2	9.9	14.4	4.6
II	9.3	9.4	11.2	5.5	7.8	10.6	7.9	7.6	7.3	8.1	9.4	12.8	15.5	6.9
III	7.6	3.8	3.8	4.8	7.8	10.0	7.3	6.8	6.7	7.2	9.3	10.2	16.0	6.6
IV	7.8	5.9	6.8	4.4	8.6	10.9	7.2	8.3	7.4	9.9	7.9	7.2	15.7	6.8
1974 I	7.5	4.6	4.2	5.6	7.5	10.2	7.4	9.1	7.6	11.3	5.7	—	15.9	7.6
II	8.5	5.9	5.7	5.7	7.4	11.1	9.4	12.1	11.4	13.2	9.4	—	15.3	8.1
Base period limit[a]	8.8	8.5	10.5	5.8	7.8	10.8	7.4	8.4	7.2	10.0	9.0	8.2	15.2	7.4

[a] Estimated for each industry by computing the average percentage profit margin for the two years in which profit margins were highest from calendar years 1968 through 1970.

Source: Federal Trade Commission, *Quarterly Financial Reports for Manufacturing Corporations*, 1968–74.

Profit margins on average moved close to base period levels in 1973, particularly in nondurable goods manufacturing. Margins rose markedly early in the year in the lumber sector (and later in the year for several other sectors) to levels apparently above base period limits. These profits data are not adjusted for inventory profits, in contrast to the data from the national income accounts discussed in the preceding section. In their treatment of inventory profits these profits data are consistent with the computational procedures in the stabilization regulations. There are several reasons, however, why these aggregate data on average profit margins for industries provide only a general indication of the degree to which realized profit margins for individual firms were consistent with the requirements for compliance with the stabilization regulations.

Comparisons of base period profit margin limits for individual firms with their realized profit margins could be significantly different from comparisons of industry averages. Individual firms could choose their most favorable two years, and, in addition, many firms use fiscal years that do not correspond to calendar years. Thus the actual difference between realized profit margins and base period limits may have been wider than would be suggested by computations based on industry sector averages for two calendar years. On the other hand, the variability of profit margins for individual firms is much larger than for the averages, and realized profit margins may exceed base period limits for some firms even though this is not reflected in an industry average.

The sales and profits data underlying published industry profit margins are also more inclusive than the data specified in the stabilization regulations. For example, subsidiaries based abroad and mainly engaged in foreign operations were excluded from profit margin computations under the stabilization regulations, and the dollar devaluations in 1971 and 1973 significantly increased reported profits for foreign subsidiaries of international corporations. Moreover, farming, life insurance, and public utilities operations were excluded if they were separate accounting entities. In general the broad definition of firms applied under the stabilization regulations also obscures comparisons with data based on different definitions.

Realized profit margins could in addition, under certain conditions, exceed base period profit margin limits without violating the stabilization regulations. During Phase II, profit margin limitations were not applied to firms that raised no prices above base period levels (prices charged in the thirty days before 15 August 1971 or on 25 May 1970). During Phase III, profit margin limits were not applied unless the firm increased prices by at least an average of 1.5 percent above levels authorized on 10 January 1973, and during Phase IV they were not applied to firms that increased no prices above levels legally prevailing during the mid–1973 freeze. A significant fraction of firms raised no prices above base period levels during 1972, and in late 1973 sales and profits attributable to exempt prices in areas such as exports, lumber, and other sectors exempted later could be excluded from profit margin computations. Firms that had increased prices, but later reduced them sufficiently to compensate for the revenue received from these price increases, were also relieved from profit margin limits. In addition, relief from profit margin limitations or adjustments to base period limits were often granted through the exceptions process. Relief of this sort reflected well-documented special circumstances experienced by a firm, circumstances such as a major change in the financial structure of the firm. The special rules applicable to firms experiencing losses or very low profits could also raise average profit margins without placing the firms at the low-profit end of the distribution in violation of the regulations. It may be concluded that the published aggregate profit margin data cannot be easily translated into evidence on the extent of compliance with the profit margin limits under the stabilization rules.

Beginning in the second quarter of 1972, orders to reduce prices and (when this was possible) to make refunds were issued to firms with profit margins exceeding base period levels. Occasionally there were denials of requests for price increases from firms approaching base period profit margin limits, with the most noteworthy cases being those for two major auto companies in late 1972. By the end of 1972, only a small number of firms showed profit margins in excess of base period limits, and they were heavily concentrated in the lumber and construction sectors. In the construction sector, the immediate linkage between profit margins and pricing was weak, and special procedures were eventually developed for construction. In other sectors remedial actions included refunds where feasible, price reductions where markets would not be unduly disrupted, or payments to the Treasury to reflect profit margin overages. In many instances the presence of special circumstances that had not been dealt with through the exceptions process led to negotiation of compromise settlements of profit margin overage problems.

The marked acceleration of price increases in early 1973 and the large increases in reported profits for the first quarter of 1973 led many observers to conclude that there was widespread noncompliance with cost-justification and profit margin regulations.[9] Yet reports on prices, costs, and profits for the first part of the year showed few instances of probable violation of the stabilization regulations.[10] In addition, since cumulative profit margins in these reports in most instances did not reflect results for a completed fiscal year, many of the apparent profit margin overages may have been attributable to seasonal factors.

Profit margin limits were applied throughout the remainder of the program, with remedies prescribed when base period limits were exceeded and denial of requests for price increases when firms were approaching base period limits. However, the sector-by-sector decontrol process during Phase IV complicated the application of profit margin limits, because exempted activities could be excluded from profit margin computations. Often only crude adjustments could be made by firms with production operations in several sectors, some of which were exempted, and application of profit margin comparisons became increasingly arbitrary and complicated during the decontrol process.

---

[9] Lack of compliance was usually implied, though not explicitly alleged, in calls for stricter controls or a return to controls similar to those of Phase II. *New York Times* editorials calling for stricter controls appeared on average more than twice a month between February and June 1973, usually immediately after wholesale and consumer price increases were announced. The *Business Week* editorial of 10 March 1973 called for a shift from "voluntary" to mandatory rules, better enforcement, and farm product price ceilings. Gardner Ackley in "And Now Phase Four" (*Dun's*, August 1973, p. 11) said that Phase III had "allowed large numbers of firms in many leading industries to violate the profit margin limitations."

[10] A preliminary review of reports covering the first four months of 1973 showed only 3 firms out of nearly 500 without adequate cost increases to support the increased revenues they had received from price increases. An internal analysis of eight industry sectors also showed price increases averaging significantly less than cost increases that had accumulated, both during the first four months of the year and by June when the freeze was imposed. By 12 July over 900 reports on costs and profits had been received from firms with annual sales of over $250 million. According to nearly 500 reports from nonfood firms that had been reviewed, price increases averaged less than 1.5 percent above levels authorized when Phase III began for about 450 firms and only 6 firms that had increased prices by more than 1.5 percent with profit margins exceeding base period levels. In the food sector only 7 out of almost 150 firms showed profit margins exceeding base period levels.

4
SECTORAL DEVELOPMENTS

During the period from 1971 through 1974 the contribution of individual sectors to inflation was highly uneven. Of course, differences in sectoral contributions to inflation reflect constantly occurring changes in relative prices for particular products and services, but differences in rates of price increase for broad classes of related products were unusually large during the last eighteen months of the controls period.

Public attention would normally be focused on sectors in which prices rose most rapidly, but the focus of public attention on food prices may have been intensified by a program of controls which was widely regarded as responsible for preventing large price increases, irrespective of developments in the marketplace. Even if they did little to increase public sensitivity to rising prices, the controls did provide a focal point toward which public dissatisfaction could be directed. Controls policies were to a large extent shaped in reaction to public and congressional pressures and in response to changes in market conditions. Consequently, review of developments in the sectors where these pressures and changes in market conditions were most important should highlight changes in controls and their effects, and sharpen our perception of the dilemma of dealing with a supposed need for aggressive use of controls despite the risk that stringent controls would disrupt markets, attenuate the allocative role of prices, and undermine efficiency.

Food

Food price performance has typically been characterized by relatively large short-term swings. Since food accounts for about one-fourth of the consumer's budget (as represented by the consumer price index) and food purchases require regular and frequent cash outlays that are not readily postponed, food prices have often been viewed as a sensitive barometer of consumers' perceptions of inflation. Thus, while food price increases were controversial from the beginning of the program, the unusually sharp rise in food prices during 1973, when they accounted for more than half of the overall rise in consumer prices, swept away the conditions necessary for the maintenance of a fragile balance between public acquiescence under flexible controls and developments in the marketplace consistent with sustaining this flexible approach.

Consumers judged controls to be ineffective because of the performance of food prices during the phases of controls in which rigid price ceilings were not in effect. Yet when the market disruption and adverse effects on supply that resulted from rigid ceilings became apparent, mainly as a result of meat price ceilings and the freeze in 1973, they contributed toward a reversal of public attitudes toward controls and to the ultimate dismantling of the program.

Background. During 1972 the food price problem at the consumer level was largely confined to meat. By 1973, however, the problem had spread to many other food products, and the overall cost level of much of the food production sector was lifted by massive grain and soybean price increases. The full effects of these developments did not become evident until later in 1973, when a combination of strong consumer demand and reduced world supplies resulted in an unprecedented surge in food prices.

Farm policy and production: 1971–72. A food price problem was not apparent during the 1971–72 crop year. After a decline in farm output in 1970 (primarily from corn blight), farm programs were liberalized significantly to reduce acreage diversion in 1971. Favorable weather also contributed to the 11 percent rise in crop output from the previous season's depressed level. World grain stocks by the end of the crop year rose by 15 percent (about 17 million metric tons) to a level of 147.7 million metric tons. Abundant supplies led to a decline in grain prices by late 1971. A sharp rise in meat and animal protein supplies, which was partly a result of the liquidation phase of the hog cycle that had peaked in late 1970 when corn prices were high (because of the blight-damaged crop), contributed to a temporary stability in meat prices.

The buildup of U.S. and world grain stocks in the fall of 1971 led to declining prices for corn and wheat, and strong farm and congressional pressures for a policy response. In the fall of 1971 the administration encouraged expanded acreage diversion under the wheat and feed grain programs, and diverted acres rose from 37.6 million in 1971 to 62.1 million in 1972. Of course 1972 was an election year, but even so, policy makers did not foresee the decline in world grain production in 1972 accompanying the programmed reduction in U.S. grain output.

World grain developments: 1972–73. A reduction in world grain output and the impact of this reduction on international markets was the major short-term force underlying the food price explosion in 1973. With reduced acreage offsetting some of the gain in yields, U.S. crop output increased by less than one percent in 1972. Adverse weather conditions, however, significantly reduced crops in the Union of Soviet Socialist Republics, China, India, Eastern Europe, Australia and Argentina. World output of wheat and coarse grains dropped 3 percent below the previous year's level and also fell below trend (Table 15). Although beginning stocks were higher than the previous year, markets were tight and prices soared.[1]

New developments on the demand side contributed to unusual pressure on world grain markets. The Soviet Union entered the U.S. grain market to compensate more fully for its reduced harvest than had been done previously,[2] and the People's Republic of China entered the U.S. grain market for the first time in many years to supplement their reduced crops.

The size of Soviet purchases in U.S. and world markets was not only unusually large, but the manner in which these sales were handled may also have contributed to the price effects of the purchases. In early July 1972 an agreement had been reached between the United States and the Union of Soviet Socialist Republics calling

---

1 Rice production fell 5 percent from the 1971 level, with the declines concentrated in the Asian countries. A wet fall in the United States delayed harvests and particularly reduced the soybean crop, and a ban on anchovy fishing in Peru reduced fishmeal production, cutting world high-protein meal supplies by 2 percent for 1972. By December 1972 the U.S. farm price for wheat, which for years had been artificially supported above world levels, had risen to $2.38 per bushel compared to $1.32 in the previous July and $1.34 in December 1971. Prices of soybean meal rose to an average of $174 per ton compared to $81 in late 1971.

2 Substantial declines in grain output in the Soviet Union had not been uncommon in the past. Wheat production in the decade of the 1960s had declined in four separate years, with the magnitudes of the drops exceeding the 1972 shortfall in absolute and relative terms. In 1963-64 when the U.S.S.R. experienced its sharpest decline in wheat production, consumption was curtailed severely and livestock herds were slaughtered to supplement diets. But in 1972 the U.S.S.R. purchased over 20 million metric tons of wheat and feed grains compared with 7.7 million tons in the previous season (13.7 million tons were purchased from the U.S. in 1972-73 and 7.9 million in 1973-74).

Table 15

TOTAL WORLD GRAIN SUPPLY-DISTRIBUTION, MARKETING YEARS 1960–61 THROUGH 1974–76

Marketing Year	Area Harvested (million hectares)	Yield (quintals per hectare)	Beginning Stocks[a] (million metric tons)	Production (million metric tons)	Total Exports[b] (million metric tons)	Consumption Total[c] (million metric tons)
1960–61	473.5	13.9	164.0	656.5	69.9	643.8
1961–62	465.7	13.4	176.7	623.7	81.5	650.4
1962–63	469.0	14.4	150.0	673.7	78.5	670.5
1963–64	475.0	14.0	153.2	664.1	94.9	669.3
1964–65	481.9	14.6	148.0	703.5	92.2	700.2
1965–66	477.1	14.9	151.3	709.2	109.0	744.9
1966–67	477.5	16.4	115.6	782.1	102.4	753.1
1967–68	485.4	16.3	144.6	791.5	98.1	776.7
1968–69	491.4	16.9	159.4	829.5	91.7	800.8
1969–70	487.1	17.1	188.1	832.1	102.4	852.0
1970–71	476.5	17.5	168.2	832.7	109.6	870.4
1971–72	484.2	19.0	130.5	920.0	114.1	902.8
1972–73	481.3	18.7	147.7	899.3	141.4	938.9
1973–74	500.6	19.5	108.1	976.6	150.3	974.7
1974–75[d]	506.8	18.2	110.3	921.0	138.0	928.3
1975–76[e]	515.6	18.2	103.0	938.4	154.7	942.6

Note: Includes wheat, rye, barley, oats, corn, and sorghum.

[a] Stocks data are based on an aggregate of differing local marketing years and should not be construed as representing world stock levels at a fixed point in time. Stocks data are not available for all countries and exclude such as the People's Republic of China and parts of Eastern Europe; the world stock levels have been adjusted for estimated year-to-year changes in U.S.S.R. grain stocks, but do not purport to include the entire absolute level of U.S.S.R. stocks.

[b] Trade data are based on an aggregate of differing local marketing years.

[c] For countries for which stocks data are not available (excluding the U.S.S.R.), consumption estimates represent "apparent" consumption, i.e., they are inclusive of annual stock level adjustments.

[d] Preliminary.

[e] Projection.

Source: U.S. Department of Agriculture, Foreign Agricultural Service.

for the Soviet Union to purchase $750 million of wheat and grain over a three-year period.[3] In early July Soviet buyers began negotiating with major private U.S. firms for wheat and feed grains and

[3] For a more complete discussion of the dramatic 1972-73 grain and oilseed events, see the August 1973 editions of the *Feed Situation* and *Wheat Situation* and the October 1973 edition of the *Fats and Oils Situation*, Economic Research Service, U.S. Department of Agriculture. See also *Milling & Baking News*, 23 October 1973.

additional large orders were placed through the fall as the deterioration in Soviet crops continued.

At the same time, even though world supply of grains was tightening, the U.S. Department of Agriculture continued to subsidize wheat exports in the traditional manner in an effort to stabilize world prices at about $1.65 per bushel. This policy continued while the price of wheat in the United States rose from about $1.50 to over $2.20.[4] The subsidy was increased from 2 cents per bushel to 47 cents before it was suspended completely in late September 1972. The continuation of the subsidy until September probably reflects the inertia of traditional practices of supporting U.S. wheat prices above world market levels and lack of recognition that radically new market conditions were emerging.

Cyclically strong demand also contributed to price pressures in U.S. and world markets for grains and animal proteins, in addition to normal demand growth attributable to population and income trends. The economies of the United States and the other major industrial countries were in a phase of strong cyclical expansion in late 1972 and early 1973. Real per capita disposable income in the United States rose exceptionally rapidly during that period (Table 16). While the expanded income growth on the surface might not appear to have been an important contributing factor, income elasticities are particularly high for red meats and therefore translate into enlarged derived demands for grain and oilseed for livestock feeds.[5] The cyclical surge in income placed an additional increment to demand on top of trend growth rates for grains of about 1.5 percent in the developed countries and 0.4 percent in the less developed countries.

Another factor that translated price pressures in world markets into unusually large price increases in the United States was the devaluation of the dollar in February 1973—the second devaluation in about a year and a half. This devaluation and further decline in the value of the dollar raised prices more in the United States than for foreign buyers seeking U.S. commodities in 1973.

The stabilization controls were administered in a context shaped by developments in world grain and animal protein markets. While numerous factors contributed to tight markets and extraordinary price increases, three were of particular importance: the Soviet wheat sale, the reduction in world grain stocks, and the relationship between

---

[4] Cash prices for #1 hard red winter wheat in Kansas City quoted in *Grain Market News*, weekly publication of Agricultural Marketing Service, Grain Division, U.S. Department of Agriculture.

[5] See Dale Hathaway, "Food Prices and Inflation," *Brookings Papers on Economic Activity*, no. 1 (Washington, D. C.: The Brookings Institution, 1974), pp. 63-116.

Table 16

DISPOSABLE INCOME PER CAPITA IN THE UNITED STATES: QUARTERLY AND ANNUAL PERCENTAGE CHANGES IN CURRENT AND CONSTANT DOLLARS, 1971–74

	Percentage Change of Per Capita Disposable Income (seasonally adjusted annual rate)				
Year	I	II	III	IV	Year
			Current Dollars		
1971	12.9	8.4	3.4	3.3	7.1
1972	7.0	7.4	8.0	5.2	6.6
1973	15.1	10.1	9.3	10.8	11.8
1974	4.1	6.2	10.6	5.5	7.6
			1958 Dollars		
1971	8.4	4.1	.3	2.1	3.1
1972	3.1	4.5	5.2	12.0	3.6
1973	9.7	1.4	1.5	0.0	6.0
1974	2.2	−1.3	−.3	−1.3	3.4

Source: *Economic Report of the President, 1975* (Washington, D. C.: U.S. Government Printing Office, 1975), p. 269, and *Economic Report of the President, 1974*, p. 269.

Table 17

RATIOS OF LIVESTOCK PRICES TO CORN PRICES: SELECTED YEARS, 1967–73

Price Ratios	**1967–71** [a]	**1972** [a]	**1973** [a]
Hog/corn	17.5	22.4	13.5
Beef-steer/corn	22.8	24.8	15.4

[a] Based on average prices for years beginning with previous October.
Source: U.S. Department of Agriculture, *Livestock and Meat Statistics*, Statistical Bulletin Number 522, July 1973, and Supplement for 1973, June 1974.

prices for grain and livestock. The Soviet wheat sale was only one element and would by itself have generated much smaller price increases than those that occurred, despite the inelastic demand for grains. Moreover, the Soviet purchases might have been substantially reduced if the subsidy program had not operated to the purchaser's benefit and if timely information on the extent of the purchases had been available. Second, the reduction in world grain stocks from

148 million tons at the beginning of 1972–73 to 108 million tons at the end of the season (Table 15) was the primary element contributing to higher grain prices. Soviet purchases amounted to over 20 million tons, with over half that amount purchased in the U.S. market. Third, the higher grain prices, which were also highly volatile in the absence of large buffer stocks, were translated into higher feed ingredient costs. Demand for meat was strong enough to support large price increases for livestock, and restoration of balance between livestock prices and feed costs required a large increase in livestock prices. The effect of the surge in grain prices on this balance is shown by the changes in livestock/feed price ratios from the 1967–71 period to ratios prevailing in 1972 and 1973 (Table 17). The change in these ratios by 1973 set the stage for the price-cost squeeze experienced by livestock producers in 1974.[6]

Food Prices and Controls Policies. Changes in retail food prices under the controls were closely linked with developments in markets for farm and food products, because limits were generally placed on processing and distribution margins instead of on food price levels. Little influence could, therefore, be exercised over food prices unless changes could be effected in domestic supply or demand in farm and food markets or unless controls were extended beyond limitations on margins. There was some use of both approaches during the stabilization program, but in view of other goals, only limited and temporary relief from food price increases was possible through more stringent controls.

Food prices through Phase II. The freeze in August 1971 produced few market dislocations, partly because seasonal declines in food prices normally occur at that time. Food price ceilings were not binding in most instances, and retail food prices declined slightly in September and October. Prices for unprocessed foods, which are more volatile than other food prices, were not subject to the freeze, and the regulations provided flexibility for seasonal price changes. Most of the problems that arose during Phase I resulted from adjustments in mandatory support prices under federal programs—such as those for peanuts, sugar, and dairy products—that forced cost absorption at processing and distribution stages.

Food prices, led by meat price increases, rose more rapidly in Phase II than did other consumer prices. Retail prices of meat, poultry, and fish rose at a 13.0 percent rate from November 1971 to January

[6] For a more detailed discussion of food price developments in 1973 and 1974, see D. Gale Johnson, *World Food Problems and Prospects* (Washington, D.C.: American Enterprise Institute, 1975), chap. 3, pp. 21-34.

1973, with the overall increase occurring in short-lived but sharp rises that generated intense concern on the part of the public and corresponding reactions by policy makers. In mid–1972, for example, when there was an increase in retail meat prices, the Price Commission was subjected to intense public criticism on the effectiveness of Phase II. There were demands for the extension of controls to raw agricultural products and the imposition of ceilings on meat prices.

A wide range of possible modifications of food price controls was considered in mid–1972. The main actions taken were a temporary suspension of meat import quotas in June following liberalization earlier in the year, and the extension of controls to distribution margins for eggs and fresh fruits and vegetables. The suspension of meat import quotas was the first clear significant action taken to increase supply in response to Cost of Living Council efforts to stabilize food prices. It was an action taken to improve the market environment for controls and thus help to maintain their credibility, and it was followed by numerous actions with a similar purpose later in the program. In this instance, as in others, the action was accompanied by other steps taken to demonstrate governmental concern—in this case including a renewed intensification of compliance auditing and enforcement activities.

Phase III and supply emphasis. The outlook for farm and food prices at the beginning of 1973 was that they would be under strong upward pressure until mid-year when livestock supplies were expected to expand and the new harvests would be brought in. Given the prospect of a disturbing rise in food prices early in the year, the council's view was that public apprehensiveness about a new phase of the stabilization program, with a significant easing of controls for most sectors, could be mitigated by a tough and visible approach to stabilization of food prices.[7] This view formed the background for the decision to retain mandatory (though slightly modified) controls in the food sector, along with procedures for policy review within the federal government to find ways to expand domestic food supplies. At the same time the procedural requirements of the controls were relaxed for most of the rest of the economy. When Phase III was introduced on 11 January 1973, a number of supply actions were announced that were designed to augment food supplies and enhance public awareness of underlying market conditions.[8]

[7] See comments on this question by George P. Shultz in *Hearings on S. 398*, pp. 17, 18, and 32.

[8] See *Economic Report of the President, 1974* (February 1974), Table 24, p. 95, for a list of these actions.

The supply actions taken in January were expected to make a marginal contribution to stabilizing the rise in farm prices that had been building up in the closing months of 1972 and to demonstrate that the government was taking action to stabilize market conditions. However, in subsequent months of 1973 farm product prices surged upward along with prices for many other commodities. Food grain prices in January were already 72 percent above January 1972 levels. During the spring, prospects for larger supplies later in 1973 were expected to be sufficient to blunt the rise in farm and food prices.[9] But by mid–1973 it had become increasingly evident that supply-demand conditions were far tighter than had earlier been expected. There was a clearer recognition by that time that a combination of short world supplies, strong international demand, and a decline in the foreign exchange value of the dollar were contributing strongly to the most explosive increase in domestic food prices since World War II.[10]

Meat ceilings. Livestock supplies fell sharply in the opening months of 1973, with beef dropping slightly and pork declining nearly two pounds per person from early 1972 rates. Consumer demand was strong, with the large income increases shown in Table 16 supporting an increase in retail beef prices of 18 percent from December to March (an annual rate of more than 90 percent).

Unable or unwilling to distinguish between the voluntary controls on nonfood commodities and continued mandatory control on food, the public and Congress blamed much of the price explosion on Phase III. Considerable pressure developed in Congress and eventually within the administration to "do something" to stop the rise in food prices, and particularly meat prices. But with per capita meat supplies in the first quarter down 4 percent from the corresponding period in 1972 and with similar reductions in poultry and egg supplies, tighter controls were a risky venture in the face of what was becoming evident—an unusually tight supply situation and continued strong demand despite consumer efforts to organize meat boycotts. With prospects for livestock supplies expected to pick up in the

9 See "Food Prices," a report prepared by the Cost of Living Council Committee on Food and released on 20 March 1973, contained in the appendix to the *Economic Stabilization Program Quarterly Report* covering the period 11 January 1973 through 31 March 1973, pp. 69-76.

10 This recognition is reflected, for example, in Secretary Shultz's statements in a White House press briefing on 18 July 1973. He made reference to a bulge in price increases after the freeze reflecting the buildup of costs in the system and declined to make any estimate of food price increases after the freeze. "Transcript of a White House Press Briefing," *Phase IV Announcement,* Economic Stabilization Program, Cost of Living Council, Washington, D. C., 19 July 1973, pp. 31-36.

second and third quarters of 1973 on the basis of available estimates, the administration on 29 March 1973 imposed ceiling prices on red meats.

The meat ceilings stopped the rise in retail beef prices, but there were other developments. Farmers curtailed marketings sharply in response to the ceilings and consumer boycott reports (Figures 6 and 7). Second quarter total per capita meat supplies dropped 6 percent from the first quarter and 9 percent from the corresponding April-June period in 1972. Per capita supplies of beef during the second quarter also dropped 9 percent from a year earlier. Actual marketing trends were in sharp contrast to a report of 1 April that indicated cattle feeders planned during April–June to expand marketings out of feedlots by 3 percent above the marketings a year earlier.[11]

Not only did cattle feeders and hog farmers cut back their marketings severely, but the ceilings squeezed packer margins causing many small plants to curtail or close operations. By August many retail chains, unable to obtain sufficient meat supplies to meet consumer wants at ceiling prices, contracted directly for custom slaughtering in order to accommodate demand. This maneuver, along with producer efforts to hold back on marketings through traditional channels, pushed up prices of live animals.

Freeze II and its effects. Despite administration efforts to tighten Phase III by placing ceilings on meat prices and more stringent rules on large nonfood firms, pressures mounted in the Congress for still further action.[12] Although ceilings on red meat prices had held livestock product prices at the farm level reasonably stable in the second quarter, rising world demand for grains and high-protein food, as well as tighter domestic supplies of fruits, vegetables, and cotton, contributed to further rises in the average level of farm commodity prices. By mid–June, the overall level of farm product prices was up 19 percent from the January 1973 level, and 38 percent from prices of the previous June. Retail food prices in June were 8.8 percent higher (unadjusted) than they were in January 1973 and 13.7 percent higher than in June 1972.

With prices sharply higher, there was rising public enthusiasm for another freeze regardless of economic conditions. Although it was not clear to the public, by late spring the market situation in the food and agricultural sector had become substantially tighter than

[11] U.S. Department of Agriculture, *Cattle on Feed*, April 1973.

[12] The unanimous vote by the Senate Democratic Caucus on 5 June 1973 to introduce legislation to impose a comprehensive ninety-day freeze and statements in favor of a freeze by powerful congressional Democrats indicate the intensity these pressures had reached.

Figure 6

SLAUGHTER RATES FOR CATTLE AND HOGS, 1972 AND 1973

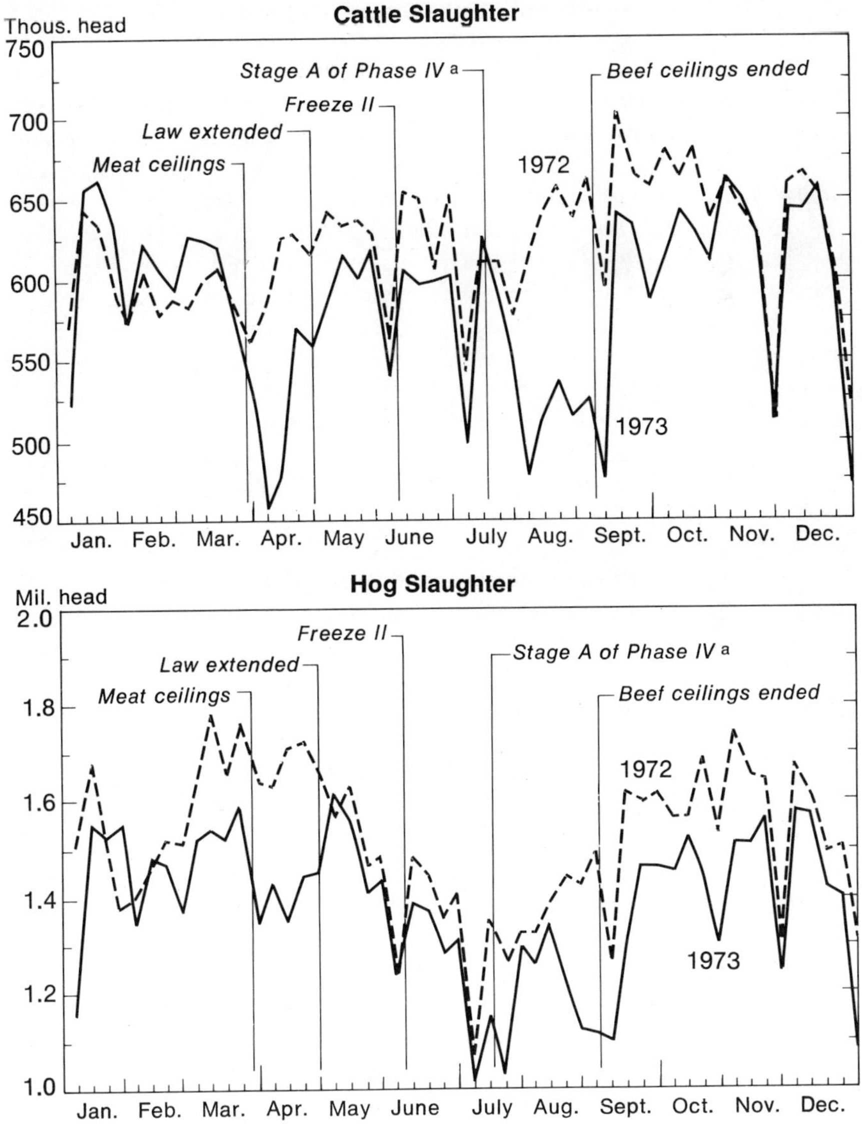

a Price ceilings on beef were continued when the freeze was lifted for the rest of the food industry by Stage A of Phase IV.

Note: Events noted in italics occurred in 1973.

Source: U.S. Department of Agriculture, Livestock Division, Agricultural Marketing Service.

Figure 7

PRICES FOR CATTLE AND HOGS, 1972 AND 1973

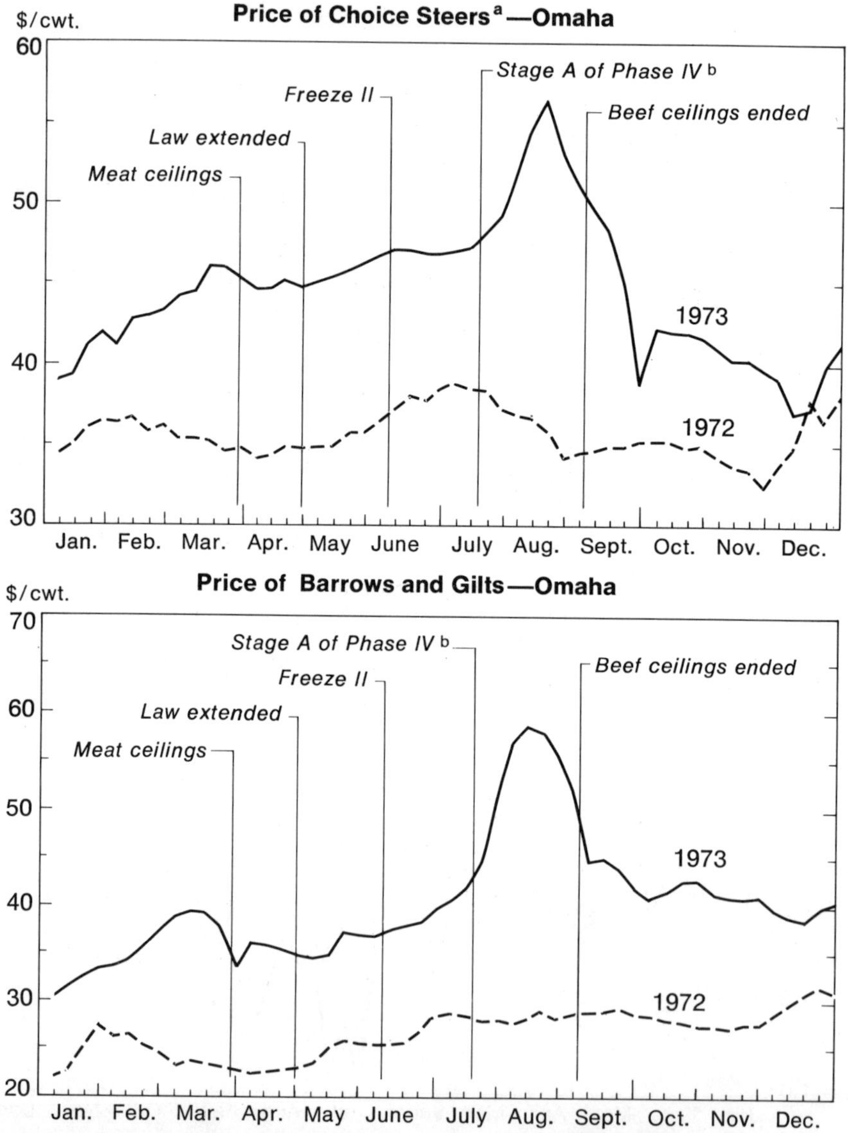

[a] Steers sold out of first hands for slaughter. Weighted averages.

[b] Price ceilings on beef were continued when the freeze was lifted for the rest of the food industry by Stage A of Phase IV.

Note: Events noted in italics occurred in 1973.

Source: U.S. Department of Agriculture, Livestock Division, Agricultural Marketing Service.

had been expected. Not only were livestock producers withholding marketings because of the meat ceilings, but the summer harvests had not yet begun. Moreover, consumer demand was running very strong. On an annual rate basis, per capita aftertax income gains in the first half of 1973 were more than double the 1972 income gain. These conditions gave rise to the possibility that supply curtailment, particularly in the food sector, might become so severe that widespread shortages and flagrant violations could force a premature end to a freeze. The momentum of public and congressional pressures, however, was not diminished by the possibility that an early retreat might be necessary. Thus on 13 June 1973, "Freeze II" was instituted. Its announced objective was to allow time for developing Phase IV, which was to be a system of flexible but "tough" controls.

Market disruptions during the second freeze exceeded the expectations of the public if not of economists.[13] Its timing was inopportune for agricultural commodities because prices generally are higher on average in July through September than in June as a result of seasonal variation in supplies. The second freeze came two months earlier in the year than Phase I, which had been instituted on 15 August. For many crops, harvest had not yet begun when the second freeze was imposed. Consequently, when new production came to market during the freeze, many processors, wholesalers and retailers were forced to sell at prices that were in effect during the first week in June—prices which in many cases reflected market conditions in the previous season. Moreover, firms could not pass on higher production costs they had incurred, and many were forced to sell at prices much below costs and market clearing levels. Shortages that appeared for particular products led some consumers to believe that food supplies were dangerously low. Newspaper articles warned of possible food shortages.[14] Support for the freeze dissolved quickly. Congress soon reversed itself; the Senate Agricultural Committee held a number of informal hearings on the severity of the market disruptions, and several bills were introduced to ease or remove controls from food prices.[15]

13 One reason why the freeze of June 1973 led to a great deal more market disruption than did the freeze of August 1971 was the change in regulations dealing with raw agricultural products. During the first freeze ceiling prices were not applied to unprocessed food products, including such products as eggs and fresh fruits and vegetables, but ceilings were applied to those products after their first sale during the second freeze since controls had been applied to distribution margins for these products in June 1972.

14 See, for example, John A. Prestbo, "Bare Cupboards," *Wall Street Journal*, 28 June 1973, p. 1.

15 See "Congress and Controls," Appendix C, section 5, *Historical Working Papers on the Economic Stabilization Program*, Part 1, pp. 226-28.

Because of the market developments and public pressure, the administration instituted "Stage A" of Phase IV for the food industry on 18 July. This "Stage A" allowed food processors, wholesalers, and retailers to adjust prices to reflect dollar-for-dollar increases in raw product costs since the first part of June in order to avoid a severe squeeze on profits in food processing and marketing firms. The price increases that followed during "Stage A" were extraordinarily large. In August farm commodity prices jumped an unprecedented 20 percent. Although the upsurge was short-lived, the results of the price pressures had some lasting effects, particularly in the U.S. livestock industry. With prices straining against ceiling levels because of reduced crop supplies and withholding of marketing by producers, consumer demand during and immediately after the freeze apparently shifted sharply upward. Consumers were apparently willing to pay higher prices for food as a result of fears of diminished food supplies aroused by the new disequilibrium that the freeze had created. Price levels of virtually all raw commodities surged to simultaneous peaks in August but fell off dramatically later in the month as demand became satisfied at new price levels (Figure 7 and Figure A-3 in the Appendix).

Although prices rose to much higher levels during the month, hog prices in August averaged over $56, choice steers at Omaha nearly $53, and feeder calves more than $72. Livestock prices consistent with ceiling prices were estimated at about $35, $45, and $53 for hogs, steers, and feeder calves, respectively. Prices for feeder calves, in particular, were bid to unwarranted levels, committing many livestock feeders to cost levels that turned their operations unprofitable once marketings picked up and put downward pressure on product prices.

A major factor in the increase in livestock prices was the administration's decision not to lift the ceilings on beef prices at the time the freeze was removed for all other food items. This caused a sharp cutback in cattle marketing and placed additional demands on competing meat supplies, adding impetus to upward price pressures. Moreover, the decision not to release beef made consumers and producers uncertain as to prices that might be sustained in the absence of ceilings. A significant decline in prices occurred during September once the ceilings on beef were removed and marketings picked up. One conclusion that can be drawn from this period is that these sharp fluctuations in supplies and prices raised the risk to producers and contributed to future instability, some of which became evident in the livestock industry in 1974. Cattle feeders and turkey and broiler producers suffered substantial losses in 1974 because of earlier overcommitments on input costs followed by sales during a period of expanding supplies, declining prices, and lower consumer demand. In the aftermath of the earlier disruptions of the industry, one result was the passage of the guaranteed credit program for livestock producers in the summer of 1974.

Meat ceilings and exports. The meat ceilings were quickly blamed for an increase in meat exports. Beginning in March 1973 exports of pork, particularly to Japan, rose dramatically. While this led to allegations that ceilings were the prime cause and speculation that domestic supplies would become more seriously affected, the data suggest that other factors were also operative. The acceleration appears to have started in March 1973, following the second devaluation of the dollar, but before the announcement of the meat ceilings (Appendix Table A-6). The surge in exports of pork dissipated in June, a month before the ceilings on pork prices were removed. Exports to Canada also rose during this period, possibly to replenish Canadian shipments to Japan. Thus while pork exports were high during much of the period when ceilings were in effect, the extent to which the rise should be attributed to exempt export sales with domestic price ceilings is unclear and the response was not of runaway proportions.

However, the meat ceilings apparently did affect live animal and meat trade with Canada. In February 1973, Canada lifted its $0.015 per pound duty on live cattle and $0.03 per pound duty on carcass beef. Because the differential between Canadian prices and U.S. prices was not sufficient to attract exports, live cattle exports to Canada lagged sharply behind the previous year. This situation changed in late July and early August. As live animal prices advanced sharply in the United States, it became increasingly difficult for U.S. slaughter plants to operate profitably under the meat ceilings. Canadian packers, however, could buy U.S. live cattle, slaughter them, and export the carcass beef back into the United States at exempt prices. During August, when custom slaughtering of beef became most prevalent in the United States, live animal shipments to Canada moved up sharply and were partially offset by a similar upsurge in dressed meat imports (Appendix Tables A-7 and A-8).

Export of live cattle to Canada remained high after U.S. meat ceilings were removed, partly because U.S. prices declined sharply when ceilings were removed. Canada, in response, reimposed the $0.015 and $0.03 duties respectively on live animals and beef on 22 September 1973. The price differential continued to be attractive, however, and in October exports reached a record high. In November the Canadian government instituted an additional $0.03 per pound duty on live animals and $0.06 on carcass beef. In late 1973 and early 1974 the depressed cattle market in the United States produced continued incentives to export to Canada in spite of higher duties, and the Canadians in April 1974 took action to ban U.S. cattle shipments on the basis that they might contain DES (a hormone used as an additive in feed). This ban was eventually lifted in August 1974, subject to certification and quotas based on 1969–72 shipment levels.

Meat specialing. Data on meat specialing, which reflect both the extent of price reductions and the proportion of sales to which the reductions applied, provide an interesting source of information on changes in business practices to offset the impact of controls. The available data are unfortunately not seasonally adjusted, which complicates analysis of month-to-month movements (Appendix Table A-9). Moreover, the analysis is clouded by the normal influence of changes in short-term supply and demand conditions.

In spite of the limitations of the data, a comparison of monthly specials with their levels a year earlier yields some interesting results. During 1972 beef specials were equal to or greater than they had been in the corresponding months in 1971 nearly half of the time. Those months during which specialing exceeded the previous year's level generally reflect large supplies and stable or falling prices. Beginning in September 1972 and continuing through February 1973, beef specials exceeded year-earlier levels every month, except for October 1972 when they were the same as in October 1971. However, in March 1973 specialing fell (red meat ceilings were imposed on 29 March 1973), and specialing continued equal to or below year-earlier levels through November of 1973. The 0.3 cent level recorded in August 1973 was the lowest level in three-and-a-half years. This low level came after ceilings on beef prices were extended when Stage A of Phase IV went into effect, and cattle prices skyrocketed to $60 per hundred weight in response to cattle feeders' cutbacks in marketings. When the beef ceilings were lifted, specialing increased. From December 1973 through all of 1974 beef specials were again larger than the same month a year earlier.

The impact of the ceilings on pork is less clear than it is on beef. In 1972, pork specialing was below 1971 levels except for two months, and in March 1973 it fell below the 1972 levels. Except for June, it remained below year-earlier levels until September. After September 1973 specials on pork remained larger than a year earlier.

While these data cannot be considered conclusive evidence, they suggest that when ceilings were in effect, retailers reduced the amount of specialing below normal levels in order to compensate in part for the lack of upward pricing flexibility.

Margins. Essentially controls were applied to processing and distribution margins in the food industry, except during periods when ceilings or freezes were imposed. Raw agricultural products were exempt during the entire period. Since information on margins is available for the food sector, it is possible to examine the behavior of those margins during the two freezes and three distinct periods of cost pass-through controls [16] from August 1971 to April 1974. The market basket components shown by program periods in Table 18, on a seasonally adjusted basis, provide aggregate information on price and margin changes. During Phase I, the impact of the freeze is reflected by a decline in the farm-retail spread and a slowdown in retail food price increases. Although farm prices actually declined during this period, seasonally adjusted farm prices rose more rapidly than they had earlier in the year.

During the entire period of controls, increases in exempt raw farm commodity prices were generally passed through to retail food prices, with margins rising gradually through 1972 and more rapidly when farm prices and other costs accelerated. Farm-retail spreads changed somewhat erratically from month to month; margins were generally compressed when farm prices first began rising sharply and temporarily widened when farm prices declined or rose less sharply. After rising only moderately during Phase II, the farm-retail spread increased much more rapidly during Phase III, as shown in Table 18. This tends to support the widespread view that Phase II was a more effective program.

The mandatory regulations applied in the food industry during Phase II, however, were continued with only limited relaxation in

---

[16] The following distinctions highlight the differences in the various phases of the controls applicable to the food industry:

Phase II. Rules were consistent with nonfood sector described earlier except that many food processors were able to qualify for volatile pricing agreements that waived prenotification requirements on raw material costs and limited the cost pass-through to dollar-for-dollar increases for categories or items.

Phase III. Rules followed Phase II except retailers were allowed to apply percentage markups to items, categories, or total food sales at the firm's option.

Phase IV. Phase III rules continued for wholesalers and retailers. Prenotification requirements were dropped for processors in favor of a gross margin restraint on raw material costs for all processing firms. Firms were allowed flexibility in choosing base periods for gross margin computation.

Table 18

MOVEMENTS IN MARKET BASKET STATISTICS BEFORE AND DURING ECONOMIC STABILIZATION PROGRAM
(seasonally adjusted annual rates)

Period	Retail Cost (percent)	Farm-Retail Spread (percent)	Farm Value (percent)
Eight months prior to Phase I (January 1971 to August 1971)	3.9	4.3	8.9
Phase I (August 1971 to November 1971)	3.2	−6.4	14.0
Phase II (November 1971 to January 1973)	8.4	1.5	17.4
Phase III (January 1973 to June 1973)	20.6	12.2	37.2
Phase IV[a] (June 1973 to April 1974)	18.1	26.9	7.4
During controls (August 1971 to April 1974)	14.4	10.8	19.7
Six months after termination of controls (April 1974 to October 1974)	5.0	3.7	8.6

[a] Includes a general price freeze from 8 June to 18 July.

Source: U.S. Department of Agriculture, Economic Research Service, National Economics Analysis Division.

their application for Phase III, raising doubts whether this could be the main source of rapid margin expansion. The temporary squeeze in margins that occurred with the sharp spurt in farm values of nearly 11 percent between November 1972 and January 1973 could have been a more important source. This possibility is supported by the fact that margins rose at a 4.4 percent rate during the first year of Phase II, through November 1972 (when margins were 1.6 percent above their average for 1972), compared to a 4.3 percent rate from November 1972 through the end of Phase III in June 1973—rates almost identical to the rise in margins in early 1971 before controls were imposed. Margins rose very sharply in late 1973 and early 1974 during Phase IV, when the food industry regulations were modified to permit almost immediate pass-through of most processing and distribution cost increases, which by that time had risen sharply from earlier levels.

Lumber

When the stabilization program began, the housing industry was in the midst of a strong cyclical recovery from its 1969–70 slump. Housing starts rose to 2.1 million units in 1971 from 1.5 million in 1970, an increase of 40 percent. Softwood lumber output rose only about 8 percent in 1971, however, and the timber cut from national forests in 1970–71 dropped 10 percent from the previous fiscal year. A large increase in net imports coupled with a drawdown in stocks enabled the lumber industry to meet demands from housing construction, although at considerably higher prices than had previously prevailed (Appendix Table A-10).

Residential construction increased further in 1972, with housing starts totaling 2.4 million units. Softwood lumber production rose only moderately in 1972 (6.0 percent), while production from the national forests increased by 14 percent in 1971–72. Although imports rose, lumber and log exports also increased, limiting the expansion of domestic supply. Timber cut from national forests accounts for about 25 percent of domestic softwood lumber production, and the failure of the federal government to adapt its supply policies to demand conditions is illustrated by the fact that there was a net increase of only 1.7 percent in supply from the national forests over a two-year period in which housing starts rose by 60 percent.

With strong cyclical lumber demand outpacing increases in available supplies during 1972, market pressures for further increases in prices were strong and lumber prices on average rose throughout most of the year. Prices charged by particular firms, however, rose by widely varying amounts because the effects of controls on individual firms were uneven. Some firms could charge relatively high prices because their prices were based on the costs of imported lumber or purchase of exempt stumpage. Fully integrated producers or firms producing under long-term stumpage contracts had small cost increases and, therefore, could increase prices only moderately. Firms approaching their base period profit margin limits were sometimes constrained from raising prices even though they were incurring higher costs. Wide discrepancies between prices quoted by particular firms for comparable products led industry trade publications to suspend reporting of some prices and to publish price ranges. The reaction in the marketplace to these conditions ranged from the development of practices to evade the controls (practices such as reduced dimensions or altered specifications to create "new products" or resales of lumber with successive application of markups) to reports of curtailed production and diversion of supplies to export markets.[17] The stabilization policy response included revocation of the small-firm exemption for lumber dealers in order to remove opportunities for arbitrage by buying at controlled prices and selling at uncontrolled prices, and in late 1972 more stringent prenotification and reporting requirements in the lumber industry.

Lumber prices continued to rise during most of 1972, but the wide differential between average domestic prices and prices of imports from Canada is evidence that lumber prices were held below market levels during Phase II.[18] The steep rise in lumber prices after Phase III began, along with the collapse in price dispersion as lumber producers applied the more flexible rules, confirms that suppression of lumber prices below market levels occurred during 1972. While development of more stringent controls was not ruled out in early 1973, the Cost of Living Council addressed the issue by engaging in a more intensive dialogue with industry representatives and establishing a high-level Lumber Task Force charged with the responsibility of obtaining commitments from the Japanese to curb imports and to expand sales of timber from the national forests.[19] The task force was able to obtain funding and commitments to boost federal timber sales in 1973, but other forces were also at work that would reduce pressures for higher lumber prices in 1973. Housing starts began to decline early in 1973 in response to the rapid rise in interest rates and the expanded housing stock after more than two years of record housing construction. By August 1973, housing starts were back to two million units. Lumber prices began declining in June 1973. When Phase IV was announced in July, the lumber industry was released from controls on the basis of improved price performance and a slackening in the supply situation. It is worth noting that despite the steps taken to expand lumber production in 1973, output actually increased by less than 1 percent for the year (although the cut from the national forests in fiscal year 1973 rose to 12.4 billion board feet,

[17] See, for example, Rinfret-Boston Associates, Inc., *Prices and Production, An Economic Analysis of Softwood Lumber and Plywood: 1970-1973* (New York, April 1974), p. 60ff., and William Poole, "Wage-Price Controls: Where Do We Go from Here?" *Brookings Papers on Economic Activity*, no. 1 (Washington, D. C.: The Brookings Institution, 1973), p. 292ff.

[18] Price spreads on the order of $35 per thousand board feet were commonly reported for standard products with domestic prices on the order of $125 per thousand board feet. Wider spreads for comparable items were frequently reported in particular cases in the last part of 1972. See *Prices and Production* by Rinfret-Boston Associates, Inc., p. 61.

[19] See "Sky-High Lumber Prices—Can Anything Be Done?" *U.S. News & World Report*, 19 March 1973, p. 39.

up 6 percent from the previous year). In addition, net imports declined in 1973. Thus, the primary factor reducing price pressures in the lumber sector seems to have been the reduction in demand as a result of a decline in residential housing construction rather than federal government supply actions (Figure 8). Federal government timber policies are, however, a significant factor in the lumber market, and responsive federal policies could contribute substantially to stabilizing lumber prices.

Petroleum Prices

A brief review of price control policies in petroleum is appropriate not only because crude petroleum prices on world markets roughly tripled by early 1974, but also because of the special features of the controls in that sector and the continuation of price controls for petroleum products under separate authority after controls in the rest of the economy were ended. The direct impact of the surge in petroleum prices on consumer prices and the importance of petroleum as an input in most sectors of the economy meant that the inflationary consequences of the increase in petroleum prices were immediate and pervasive. Sharp increases in petroleum company profits at the same time heightened political sensitivity to the price issue. Only an outline of events is given here to avoid obscuring the general approach in a detailed technical treatment of petroleum price controls.[20]

Petroleum prices on world markets rose above domestic price levels in early 1973. Since imports accounted for about one-third of domestic petroleum consumption, failure to permit price increases so that increased import costs could be passed through would threaten a serious reduction in imports, and therefore in domestic supply. Moreover, since imported petroleum products were generally not physically distinguishable from domestically produced products, there would be strong pressures for prices of domestically produced products to rise to world market levels.

Mandatory regulations permitting only limited pass-through of increased costs were placed on the largest petroleum companies in March 1973. By mid-year it was clear that more complex and comprehensive regulations would need to be developed unless all domestic prices were permitted to increase to match rapidly rising world prices.

[20] A discussion of petroleum price control policy during the first year of special regulations for that sector is contained in "History of Petroleum Price Controls," *Historical Working Papers on the Economic Stabilization Program,* Part 2, pp. 1223-1340.

Figure 8

INDEX OF RELATIVE WHOLESALE PRICES OF SOFTWOOD LUMBER AND LEVELS OF NEW PRIVATE HOUSING STARTS, 1958–74

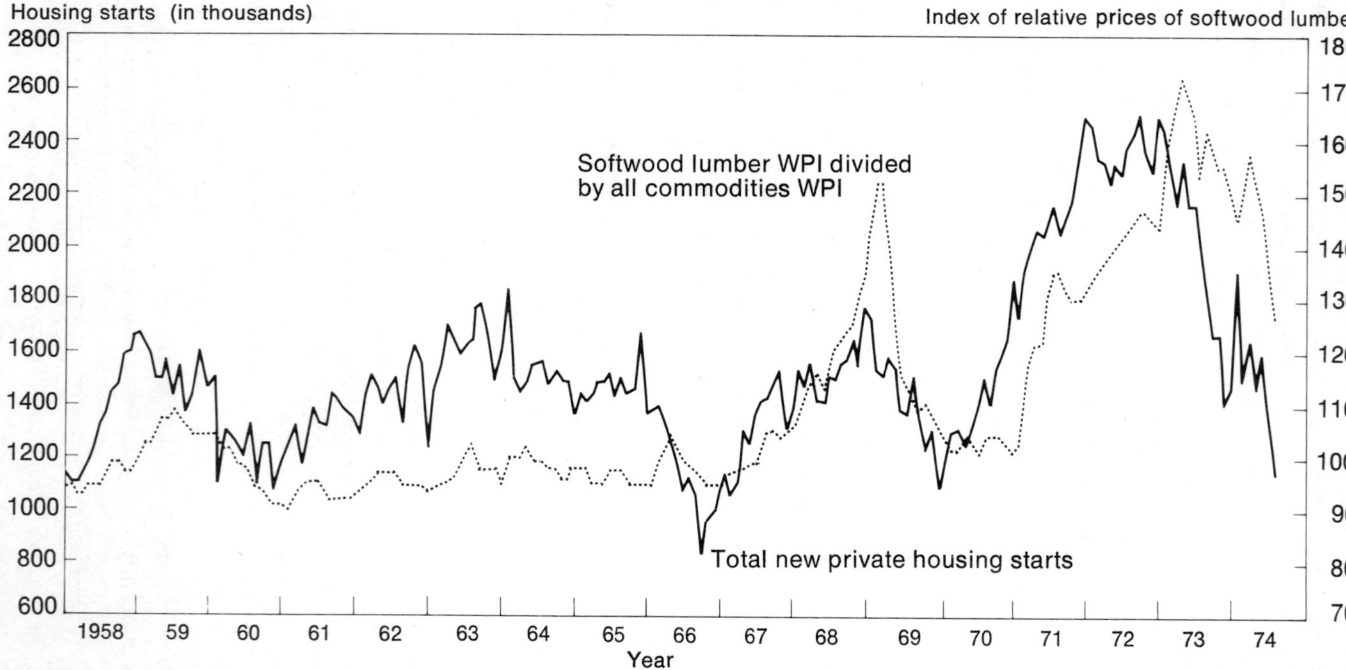

Source: Bureau of Labor Statistics, Wholesale Price Index Division; U.S. Department of Commerce, Bureau of the Census, Construction Statistics Division.

The system of controls that was developed and applied in August 1973 was relatively simple in concept but complex in application. There were difficulties in establishing cost increases for companies with integrated production, transportation, refining and sales operations; complicated patterns of sales and exchanges of crude and refined products among companies; and diversity of energy, fertilizer and petrochemical products that were affected. The substantive effect of the system was to keep average domestic prices below marginal costs of imported petroleum to the U.S. economy.

Price ceilings on domestically produced crude petroleum were the central element in the controls system. Holding prices for domestically produced crude petroleum below world market price levels significantly reduced the total cost increases that would otherwise have been passed through to price increases throughout the refining and distribution system. To encourage increased domestic production, no control was exercised over production exceeding a specified base level, and to augment the incentive for increased production an equivalent amount of oil production within base levels was removed from control if production was increased. (Production from small stripper wells was exempted later by congressional action.) The price level for domestically produced crude oil that was removed from controls was essentially indeterminate over a broad range because of possibilities for arrangements to tie in sales of controlled and uncontrolled oil. Practices of this sort apparently did not become prevalent however, because of an implicit threat of imposition of ceilings if prices of exempt domestically produced oil rose above world market levels and because buyer-seller arrangements for old oil were frozen in late 1973. Increased costs of imported crude oil and of domestic oil not subject to controls could be passed through to the consumer level at intervals, along with periodic increases in margins to offset reduced volume during the embargo in the winter.[21]

The controls on petroleum product prices kept prices significantly below levels that would otherwise have been reached during the embargo, and of course the reduced supplies of petroleum were accompanied by shortages and conservation measures in addition to

21 The initial approach of the regulations published in August delayed pass-through of cost increases at the retail level for gasoline, diesel fuel, and heating oil compared to price increases to reflect increased costs incurred by refiners and importers of petroleum products. This approach was quickly challenged in the courts and Congress as well as through publicity efforts raising the threat of strikes by the retail service station operators who were sufficiently numerous to make their influence felt. Instead of squeezing retail margins and exerting back-pressure on the pricing policies of the large oil companies, the controls, in fact, led to retail margins that rose by about 25 percent during 1973.

higher prices. With prices below market levels, a mandatory allocation system was devised in an effort to equalize the degree of shortages both geographically and within the production sector. While an adjustment of one dollar was made to domestically produced crude oil price ceilings during the winter, the price ceilings held crude oil prices for somewhat over half of domestic consumption at about half the level of world market prices in early 1974.

Petroleum product shortages, particularly for gasoline, were highly visible during the embargo. The large price increases that occurred were not sufficient to curb consumption to the level of the suddenly reduced supplies. It is clear that petroleum prices would have surged much more strongly than they did had there not been controls, and that the adjustment costs in the economy from price increases sufficiently large to ration available supplies during the embargo would have been unusually severe. It is also clear, however, that—through the imposition of price ceilings to reduce the price surge—the controls also helped to sustain domestic levels of petroleum products usage, and the petroleum-exporting countries were beneficiaries of the higher consumption levels and lower average prices prevailing in the U.S. economy. The cartel of major petroleum-exporting countries was able to maintain further increases in crude petroleum prices during 1974 by curtailing production to levels consistent with import demands.[22]

Cattle Hides

Cattle hides provide an interesting example of a commodity that during the early stages of the controls received a disproportionately large share of attention relative to its importance in the overall economy. In the spring of 1971, Argentina imposed export controls on hides. These controls significantly reduced their supply in international trade. Markets for hides were also affected by the imposition of Phase I in August 1971. When they experienced difficulty in obtaining supplies at base prices, U.S. tanners stepped up lobbying efforts for export controls (their efforts had been successful in 1966).[23] After Phase II began, domestic supplies were adequate but prices were sharply higher. In 1972 prices continued to rise, reaching an average

[22] See Richard B. Mancke, *Performance of the Federal Energy Office* (Washington, D. C.: American Enterprise Institute, 1975) for an evaluation of price and allocation controls during the embargo.

[23] See John Sheahan, *The Wage-Price Guideposts* (Washington, D. C.: The Brookings Institution, 1967), pp. 71-72 for a discussion of actions in this sector during the period of the guideposts.

level more than double that of 1971, and contributing 1.1 percent to the rise in wholesale industrial prices for the year even though they accounted for only .246 percent of the industrial component of the index.

In response to the large increases in hide prices relative to other commodities, considerable time in Phase II was devoted to analyzing and debating alternative policy strategies to cope with the U.S. leather industry's problem. The Price Commission modified its regulations to limit the pass-through of leather manufacturers' costs to dollar-for-dollar price increases, and in mid-1972 the Department of Commerce imposed export limitations to stem the outflow of hides from U.S. markets. This latter action, however, was quickly reversed in response to counter-lobbying by cattle producers who convinced the Congress that export controls were detrimental to their interests.

It is worth noting, in view of the concern the issue elicited during 1972, that hide exports increased only 10 percent over the previous year, and exports in the previous year had been affected by a dock strike (Appendix Table A-11). Moreover, after their peak in November 1972, hide prices declined and continued downward during the commodity price explosion of 1973 despite a reduction in U.S. cattle slaughter. Prices of hides did, however, rise temporarily during post-Freeze II "bulge" in August 1973 when cattle were withheld from marketing.

Fertilizer

Following a period of excess capacity in the late 1960s, the controls caught the fertilizer industry in a changing posture as worldwide demand pressures were moving into closer balance with production capacity. Prices paid by farmers for anhydrous ammonia had reached their lowest level in late 1969 and early 1970 after declining for several years. Prices then turned upward and fertilizer markets were tightening by the time Phase I was launched. The industry's petition for relief from controls in late 1971 maintained that the base period for profit margin limits established during a period of sluggish performance in the late 1960s unfairly penalized the fertilizer industry. Although relief from controls was denied, many firms were granted additional pricing flexibility by the Price Commission.

It is difficult to determine whether the controls held fertilizer prices significantly below market clearing levels during Phase II. Despite the moderate size of the increase in retail prices, domestic use rose only slightly in fiscal year 1972 and farmers experienced no

Figure 9

CORN YIELD RESPONSE TO NITROGEN APPLICATIONS

(Indiana, 1967–69)

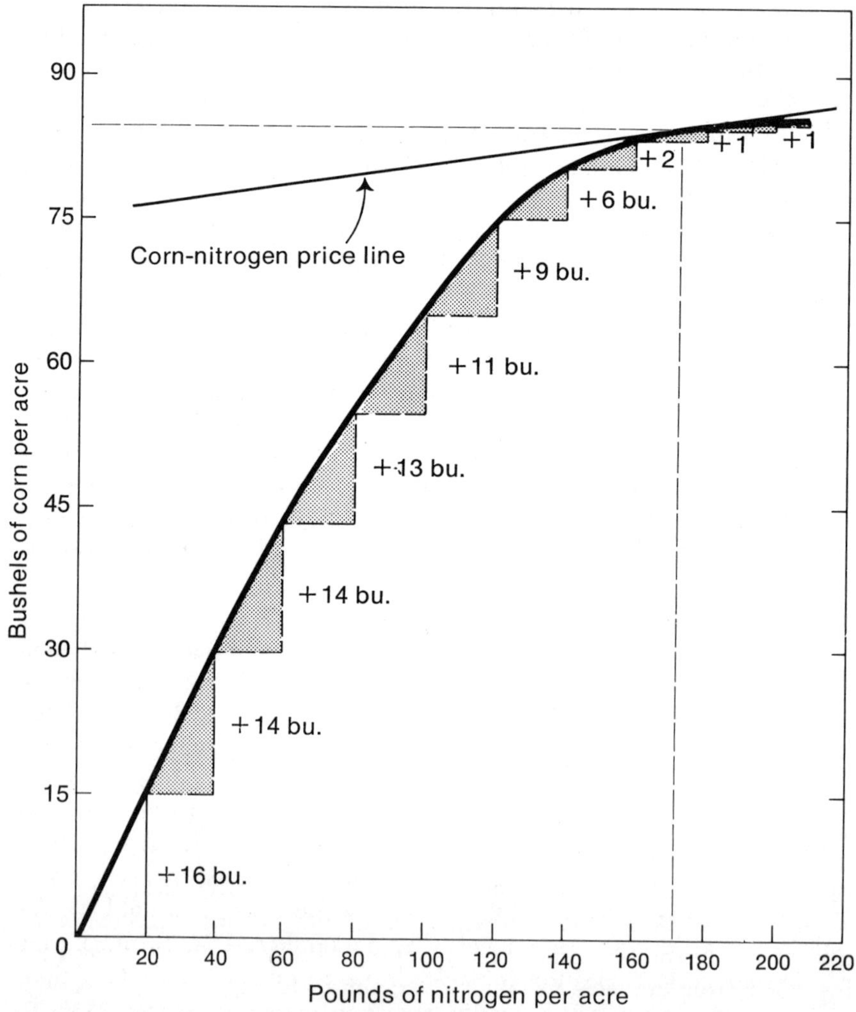

Note: The corn-nitrogen price line shows the relationship between the price of corn and the price of nitrogen in 1974. (Corn at $3.50 per bushel and nitrogen at 20¢ per pound yields a ratio of 3.50/.20 = 17.5.) At these relative prices the optimal rate of nitrogen application is slightly over 170 pounds per acre. In 1973 the price ratio was about 26.6 implying an optimal application rate about 10 pounds higher than in 1974. Actual application rates in Indiana, however, were 124 pounds and 113 pounds in 1972 and 1973, respectively.

Source: John T. Martin, "How Much Can You Afford to Pay for Nitrogen?" *Purdue Farm Management Report,* April 1974, p. 2.

major difficulties in obtaining supplies. However, the large increase in diverted acres in 1972 held down demand. In late 1972 and early 1973 the rise in grain prices, coupled with the relaxation in acreage diversion, raised the demand for fertilizer. The fertilizer market began to tighten significantly by mid-1973 when grain prices relative to fertilizer prices made increased fertilizer usage especially attractive. Figure 9 shows that at prevailing relative prices, application rates were still below optimal levels, making fertilizer an attractive input.

During the summer and fall of 1973, grain prices were rising and fertilizer prices were subject to controls, and as a consequence, increased fertilizer usage became particularly profitable to farmers in seeding wheat for harvest in 1974 (Table 19). Farmers found that traditional fertilizer dealers were no longer able to meet their needs. Dealers began to cut off slow-paying customers, credit sales became more difficult to obtain, and distribution channels were generally in a state of flux. The fertilizer industry again petitioned the Cost of Living Council for release from controls, arguing that since agricultural production had been completely released from acreage controls for 1974, the fertilizer industry should have the flexibility to meet this demand. The industry further argued that because world prices were higher than prices which could be cost-justified domestically, there was an enormous incentive to sell abroad.

The expansion of food supplies was a major objective of policy makers in 1973 and 1974, and fertilizer—a major input into the food production system as opposed to a consumer item—therefore became an early candidate on the decontrol agenda.[24] Controls were lifted from the fertilizer industry in October 1973 in return for commitments from the companies to expand production and reduce planned shipments into export channels. Fertilizer prices in both domestic and world markets rose sharply after decontrol. By 15 April 1974, anhydrous ammonia was selling to farmers for $183 per ton, even though manufacturers had been asked by the council to hold wholesale prices at January 1974 levels. By September 1974, farmers were paying about $229 per ton for anhydrous ammonia (Table 19). Spot prices on world markets for many products were quoted in a $350- to $400-per-ton range in 1974 (Table 20).

One of the effects of the lifting of controls on fertilizer was a transfer of income from U.S. farmers to fertilizer manufacturers. However, if the controls had remained in effect and U.S./world price differentials had widened further with rising world market prices,

---

[24] See "Why Fertilizer Is in Such Short Supply," *Business Week*, 6 October 1973, p. 84.

Table 19

PRICES OF CORN, WHEAT, AND ANHYDROUS AMMONIA FERTILIZER, 1970–74

	Prices				
	1970	1971	1972	1973	1974
Wheat ($ per bushel)[a]	1.33	1.34	1.76	3.95	4.04
Corn ($ per bushel)[a]	1.33	1.08	1.57	2.55	2.95
Anhydrous ammonia ($ per ton)[b]	76.80	79.30	80.80	92.50	229.00

[a] Prices received by farmers (crop year).

[b] Prices paid by farmers on 15 September.

Source: U.S. Department of Agriculture, Statistical Reporting Service, *Agricultural Prices, Annual Summary,* June 1974 and June 1975 issues.

Table 20

COMPARISON OF DOMESTIC (U.S.) AND EXPORT PRICES OF GRANULAR TRIPLE SUPERPHOSPHATE AND DIAMMONIUM PHOSPHATE

($/net ton f.o.b. Tampa, Florida)

Year Ending 30 June	U.S. Price[a]		Export Price[b]		$/Ton Differential	
	TSP[c]	DAP[d]	TSP	DAP	TSP	DAP
1969	48.30	66.30	35.65	n.a.	12.65[e]	n.a.
1970	42.15	58.10	46.19	53.08	4.04	5.02[e]
1971	40.85	56.45	53.48	51.52	12.63	4.93[e]
1972	42.35	58.30	50.82	75.77	8.47	17.47
1973	47.20	64.90	82.60	96.80	35.40	31.90
1974	120.00[f]	150.00[f]	290.30[g]	353.80[g]	170.30	203.80

[a] C.f. industries, net selling price to member, f.o.b. Tampa.

[b] Award prices on exports as reported by International Commodities Export Corp., f.o.b. Tampa.

[c] TSP—triple superphosphate.

[d] DAP—diammonium phosphate.

[e] In favor of U.S. price.

[f] Estimated.

[g] ICEC reports of June and August 1974.

Source: U.S. Department of Agriculture, Economic Research Service, National Economics Analysis Division.

supplies available for domestic usage might have been significantly reduced. In addition, less efficient distribution among domestic users and more widespread shortages might have reduced total crop output in 1974.

The sharp rise in fertilizer prices contributed to a worldwide flurry of planned additions to plant capacity. Continuation of domestic controls might have discouraged domestic investment in additional fertilizer production capacity, and diversion of U.S. production to export markets might have delayed expansion in other countries if prices and supplies on world markets were significantly affected. It is also possible that this capacity might have come on stream sooner if the controls had not previously held prices down. However, federal and state regulation of natural gas prices complicates an assessment of the influence of price controls on investment decisions. Moreover, the cyclical nature of the fertilizer industry—related partially to world grain movements—also complicates assessment of the effects of controls on production and investment decisions in the industry. It is likely, however, that domestic supplies would have been lower and the incidence of shortages more severe in 1974 in the absence of decontrol of fertilizer and the large price increases that followed.

Other Sectors

Among the other sectors in which marked policy changes occurred in the application of controls, the most important were health services and rents for residential units. Regulations were specially tailored to the economic and institutional characteristics of each sector. For health services the main features of the regulations were a system of ceilings on increases in physicians' and other professional fees and crude limits on revenue increases obtained by raising rates for hospital care. Although the health services controls were even more deficient in taking into account changes in costs and services than the controls that were applied in most other sectors, a significant deceleration in the rise in health services prices occurred during the stabilization program. A more carefully tailored system for controlling health services costs was developed during 1973, and continuation of controls beyond 30 April 1974 was initially requested only for this sector.

Control of residential rents was important both because of the disproportionately large share of resources that were devoted to compliance and enforcement activities and because of its political appeal. The strength of political forces favoring rent control became evident when all rents that remained under control were exempted under Phase III in 1973, and reimposition of rent controls through congressional action was narrowly averted.

By mid–1973, controls were impinging on normal market processes in a wide range of industry sectors, market situations, and individual firms. The growing incidence of market pressures pushing prices to levels at which they were constrained by controls transformed the character of policy actions in administering the program. Greater emphasis began to be placed on administering existing regulations to limit disruptive effects on markets for particular sectors and firms. Resolution of microeconomic issues, consequently, was given more attention than were broad changes in the regulations. A comprehensive survey of the conditions in, and influences of controls policy on, particular markets or submarkets would require data much more detailed than those currently available. However, examples of some of the ways in which controls influenced market efficiency are summarized in the following chapter.

5
CONTROLS AND EFFICIENCY

The concept of efficiency is central to economics, and the general principle that competitively determined prices and wages are consistent with efficient resource usage is well known. Failure to achieve full efficiency in resource usage results from production and consumption decisions based on price and wage relationships that differ from those that would prevail in competitive markets. Failure to achieve full efficiency may occur because markets are not fully competitive or because of market imperfections such as externalities in which costs or returns are not fully reflected in prices. Government regulatory practices and standards, although they are frequently designed to limit the effects of market imperfections, may sometimes contribute instead to reduced efficiency if they are applied with a rigidity that reduces competition, distorts production and pricing decisions, or discourages supply. General controls on prices and wages also have the potential for imposing serious costs on the economy by reducing efficiency.

Price and wage controls can give rise to inefficient resource usage, because suppression of price and wage levels also usually influences interrelationships between them. Controls can introduce inefficient business practices, and lead to patterns of resource usage that add to inefficiency arising from existing market imperfections. Moreover, their influence is extended over a major share of the economy. The magnitude of the costs that may be imposed by controls is not easily estimated, but constantly changing conditions in the marketplace make it virtually impossible to manage a system of stringent controls without creating distortions in resource usage. Particular instances of market disruptions, misalignment of prices, wasteful business practices, or inequitable wage relationships resulting from controls have usually become evident, but public reaction to these costs builds slowly because most of the costs are hidden and not easily quantified.

Considerations of efficiency are usually given primary emphasis in economic analyses of market problems and policies. It must be recognized, however, that the cost of distortions resulting from controls should be weighed against costs of price or wage adjustments that would occur without controls. For example, costs of occasional shortages of meat, inefficient allocation of meat consumption, and confusing price signals to producers should be weighed against the prospect that a large short-term rise in retail meat prices could raise the level of future wage adjustments, thereby building in longer-term inflation that would need to be offset later by restrictive demand management policies that would depress production. There are also serious costs that result from rapid adjustment to large short-term price changes. For example, the cost of short-term adaptation to a surge in energy costs may be extremely high compared to adjustment costs over a longer term during which existing investment can be modified or replaced to reflect a new pattern of relative prices. Finally, considerations of equity as well as efficiency are important, particularly for wages and income distribution, and the temporary departures from efficiency that may result from controls may be worthwhile if the time they provide for adaptation relieves apparent inequity and reduces social tensions or labor strife.

Unfortunately, most of the evidence on distortions resulting from controls is fragmentary and anecdotal in character and does not lend itself to quantification of the costs that result from such distortions. Yet the symptoms of inefficiency were sufficiently pervasive and their potential cost sufficiently important to merit a brief general discussion of the problem in addition to that contained in the preceding sections.

Symptoms of Inefficiency

During the first year of controls, there was some evidence that controls were interfering with the price adjustments necessary to maintain efficiency and avoid shortages, but the evidence was limited mostly to the lumber sector and to a small number of situations in which pricing to reflect increases in current production costs led either to dispersion in prices for similar products or to prices too low to satisfy current demand.[1] The stabilization regulations were based on the idea that price adjustments should be allowed to reflect cost increases, with shifts in demand in most instances expected to be accommodated

[1] For example, sugar and certain other food products prices were differentially affected by technical details of the regulations, and modifications in the regulations or exceptions for particular firms were made to alleviate these situations.

through changes in output. It became apparent in the early months of the program, however, that situations would arise in which application of the regulations would forestall some price increases that were necessary to maintain efficiency.[2]

In markets with relatively inelastic supply, short-term demand changes that were large relative to short-term cost increases created one class of problems under cost pass-through regulations. Shipping rates for ocean tankers, typically characterized by wide fluctuations in response to demand changes, on average were rising in early 1972. Many individual tankers could obtain rates in the market exceeding those received for particular shipments during the base period, but under the regulations they could not charge higher rates because costs had not increased. Pricing of radio and television advertising had traditionally reflected shifts in audience ratings of shows in addition to more stable factors, and these demand-related changes were not accompanied by short-term cost changes. Since export prices were exempt from controls, demand increases for internationally traded products created incentives to export and opportunities to earn windfall profits for traders buying at controlled domestic prices and exporting at higher world prices.

Differences among industries and among the structures of firms within industries sometimes complicated the application of cost pass-through regulations. In the case of sugar, some fruits and vegetables, and later of lumber, vertically integrated firms often experienced no short-term cost increases that could be used to justify higher prices, while other firms purchasing inputs such as raw agricultural products and standing timber in exempt markets were bidding up raw material input costs and raising prices proportionately. The presence of large inventories in some cases also weakened the linkage between cost increases and current demand conditions. For sectors engaged in processing and distribution of food products, changes in demand or supply usually were quickly reflected in changes in costs and prices throughout the production and distribution chain. In some sectors in which prices of major inputs were not exempt, short-term demand increases created an incentive for firms to increase current operating costs (such as wages), both to provide the basis for price increases and to avoid increasing profits above base period levels. The importance of this indirect influence on wages in the economy is uncertain,

[2] During the first week of Phase II, for example, rising cattle prices, with the largest meat-packing firms subject to prenotification and a delay of up to thirty days for price increases, showed the need for special provisions for inputs with volatile prices in order to avoid market disruption and markedly different treatment of large and small firms.

but one case in the textile industry in which a wage adjustment was apparently motivated mainly by profit margin considerations was brought to the attention of the Cost of Living Council in 1973.[3]

The problem of prices on world markets rising above prices permitted under domestic controls, stimulating increased exports, first appeared for cattle hides during the ninety-day freeze. When similar conditions developed in the silver market, silver was exempted from controls, but no further exemptions were made during 1972 even though world prices moved above domestic prices for several products (such as lumber, zinc, and molasses), and prices on international markets were rising and often approaching domestic price levels for a broad range of products. While rising prices on world markets posed few difficulties for domestic price controls during 1972, the surge in dollar prices of most commodities traded in international markets during 1973 (including the prices of metals, petrochemicals, and fertilizer) posed problems for any system of domestic controls.

Extension of controls to raw agricultural commodities would have created similar problems in that sector. The stringent limits on domestic prices after the June 1973 freeze, with world prices continuing to rise, threatened diversion of domestically produced supplies to export markets. Exemption from domestic controls was granted for commodities such as copper scrap and a number of other nonferrous metals. Prices of fertilizer and petrochemical products were also exempted so as to reduce incentives for trade diversion, and price adjustments to levels above those generally permitted under the standards were granted for other commodities such as copper and aluminum.[4]

When prices of more and more commodities were held below market clearing levels in late 1973, symptoms of inefficiency became increasingly widespread and diverse. Curtailment of domestic supply was sometimes threatened by increased exports, reduced production to avoid losses, and failure to expand production through use of marginal production capacity. Lack of availability and wide differences in prices of material inputs complicated production planning and threatened to disrupt production schedules. Distribution and purchasing operations were complicated by multiple prices and instances of bartering in order to reduce costs or obtain scarce

[3] In this case, as in many others, the matter was brought to the attention of the Cost of Living Council informally, and it was dealt with without the need for formal action.

[4] See, for example, Sidney Fish, "Controls Spur Exports of Scarce Commodities," *Journal of Commerce*, 14 December 1973, p. 1.

materials, and black markets were frequently reported.[5] Shortages were perhaps the most commonly reported symptom of inefficiency, although it was often difficult to distinguish between shortages and other symptoms in the absence of general price ceilings. Such distortions were instrumental in shaping public attitudes toward decontrol.

Cost Pass-Through and Product Mix

Limiting price increases to cost increases, instead of controlling overall processing margins with complete flexibility in relative prices, in some circumstances exacerbated shortages for certain products. For industries operating at capacity levels, incentives to shift the mix of products were created under regulations that linked price increases to cost increases, without permitting increases in some prices to offset reductions in others. These incentives were created even though full pass-through of cost increases was permitted, and price increases to reflect these cost increases could be spread over a broad range of product lines. For cyclical reasons and because of changes in import competition or other factors, profitability of individual product lines may diverge from that of other product lines produced by the same firm. When conditions changed and demand was sufficiently strong to support expanded production of relatively more profitable lines, incentives were created for shifting production toward high-margin product lines and for raising prices for these product lines to the extent justified by overall cost increases.

During 1973 when demand levels pressed strongly on available production capacity, there were several industries in which shortages became severe for product lines that had previously been produced at low profit margins. Some users were forced to switch to higher quality paper when lower quality paper became unavailable.[6] Some of the most marked steel shortages were in product lines such as concrete reinforcing bars, mining roof bolts, and baling wire, which had earlier been subject to strong import competition. A wide range

[5] Such instances were frequently reported on the basis of surveys by the National Association of Purchasing Managers and in trade publications and newspapers. Some instances in sectors such as petrochemicals and plastics and nonferrous metals are discussed in the *Economic Stabilization Program Quarterly Report* covering the period 1 October 1973 through 31 December 1973, chapter 2, pp. 5-34. See also Herbert Koshetz, "Black Market in Textile Yarns Is Seen," *New York Times*, 15 January 1974, p. 49.

[6] The case of paper is listed among the "proven" distortions in Appendix Q of *Statement of John T. Dunlop*, p. A-114.

of petrochemical inputs and products produced by petroleum refiners were in extremely short supply, after a period in which prices in the chemical industry had been cyclically depressed. The shortages of petrochemical feedstocks were particularly noteworthy, because allocation of a disproportionate share of cost increases to these products was encouraged by the regulations which delayed price increases for gasoline, diesel fuel, and home heating oil.

Shortages

Reports of shortages were pervasive in late 1973, and the reports often attributed shortages to the price controls.[7] Shortages are the inevitable counterpart of controls that keep prices below market clearing levels in a simple, static, analytical framework, and the existence of shortages is prima facie evidence that controls are binding. Shortages have sometimes emerged, however, in strong cyclical expansions, and phenomena such as lengthening order backlogs, slower delivery schedules, and temporary unavailability of products or materials have been quite common. Thus in an environment with rapidly changing supply conditions and strong cyclical demand, shortages and related phenomena may be partially attributable to concern with customer-supplier relationships expressed through maintenance of relative stability in materials availability and prices.

Nevertheless, controls can exacerbate shortages by influencing demand and available supply. If controls are generally thought to be holding prices below market levels, the risk of a decline in prices of materials purchased as inputs and temporarily held in inventory is reduced, and the potential for implicit capital gains if prices are decontrolled or price increases are granted is enhanced. In addition, controls that effectively constrain prices increase the probability that essential materials or products may not be available when they are needed. This encourages users to purchase materials before they are needed and hold them temporarily in inventory as a hedge against possible disruption of production schedules. Legal limits on prices

[7] Shortage situations were widely reported in trade publications and in the news media in late 1973 and early 1974. Widespread concern about the incidence and causes of shortages led to three major surveys in late 1973 by the National Association of Purchasing Managers, the National Association of Manufacturers, and the National Association of Business Economists. Long lists of materials in short supply were reported in each, and shortages and black markets were frequently attributed to the controls. See also "Managing in a Shortage Economy," *Business Week*, 10 November 1973, p. 150, and "More and More Scarcities: Who Is Feeling the Pinch," *U.S. News & World Report*, 3 September 1973, p. 15.

foreclose the possibility of bidding up prices to obtain essential materials when those materials are immediately necessary to maintain production schedules or to avoid delays.

If purchasing policies were significantly influenced by controls in this manner, these policies would have raised demand above normal current production requirements for products and materials in which the difference between price limits and market prices was largest and the potential for shortages greatest. A tendency for inventory build-up would be expected, although it might not necessarily be reflected in normal inventory data. It might be reflected in somewhat earlier purchases of supplies and materials by final users instead of larger inventories for manufacturers and distributors.

The pattern of inventory accumulation for all manufacturers and distributors indicates that firms were generally attempting to increase inventories in late 1973 and early 1974, even though serious shortages and prices significantly below market levels were concentrated in a limited range of basic materials and products. There were widespread reports of particular instances in which advance material purchases were made and purchasing practices were tailored to shortage conditions. There were reports from construction firms of advance delivery of concrete reinforcing bars to avoid costly delays in projects should these materials not be available on schedule.[8] In the petroleum products area, there were reports of a build-up of propane inventories and gasoline storage, and gasoline stocks rose toward the end of each month in anticipation of the granting of new price increases.[9] There were also reports of purchases of certain scarce materials for use in bartering for other materials in short supply because prices were kept below market levels.

In 1973 price ceilings applicable to individual firms instead of industry-wide price ceilings may have increased incentives for acquiring inventories in excess of immediate production needs. Firms having established relations with suppliers constrained by low price ceilings had a strong incentive to take delivery of all supplies that they were allocated, because prices from alternative sources of supply were often higher and further price increases were being granted

[8] These practices were reported by construction contractors, who frequently preferred higher prices to shortages. See, for example, "Builders Warn: No Rebars, No Building," *Business Week*, 8 December 1973, p. 37, and Michael K. Drapkin, "Steel Concrete-Reinforcing Bar Shortage May Severely Hurt Nonresidential Building," *Wall Street Journal*, 21 January 1974, p. 24.

[9] The behavior of inventories is emphasized in Richard B. Mancke's analysis of the influence of petroleum price controls in *Performance of the Federal Energy Office*.

periodically. In the fall of 1973, for example, price ceilings for domestic copper producers were $.60 per pound. Moreover, fabricated copper products could be priced on the basis of costs ranging from $.60 per pound for domestically produced copper or $.77 per pound for copper scrap to over $1.00 per pound for spot market purchases of imported copper. Similar conditions prevailed for other nonferrous metals such as zinc, lead, and aluminum as well as for a variety of steel and petrochemical products.[10]

It is extremely difficult to distinguish between the influence of controls and the influence of cyclical factors on the widespread incidence of shortages in 1973. The changes in market conditions resulting from shifts in supply or demand were the underlying forces creating pressures for either higher prices or shortages. It is possible that the controls themselves made an independent contribution to the problem by raising demand for inventories, reducing domestic supply through diversion to export markets, and weakening price incentives to expand production. Broad indicators—such as unfilled orders and the ratio of unfilled orders to shipments—were cyclically strong, but they may themselves have been influenced by the existence of controls. While the unusual pervasiveness of shortages in 1973 is strong evidence that controls contributed to their severity, the controls may in addition have made shortages more visible by providing a focal point for public attention.[11]

Business Practices

There are various ways in which the controls may have altered business practices and decisions in addition to their direct influence on prices. It is difficult to judge the importance of these effects either for their short-term costs or for their longer-term influence. Some effects, such as changes in accounting practices to obtain greater flexibility for price increases or changes in production methods or product mix, mainly involve short-term costs. The costs of other

[10] Changes in the spread between prices on domestic and world markets between 1 January 1973 and 30 November 1973 for aluminum, copper, lead and zinc are shown in *Economic Stabilization Program Quarterly Report* covering the period 1 October 1973 through 31 December 1973, p. 31.

[11] For discussions of specific instances of shortages and inefficiency that were attributed to controls in a wide range of industry sectors, see the statements and testimony of representatives from the private sector in Hearings before the Subcommittee on Production and Stabilization of the Senate Committee on Banking, Housing and Urban Affairs, *Oversight on Economic Stabilization* and *Economic Stabilization Act—1974*, 93d Cong., 2d sess. (30 and 31 January, 1, 6, 19, and 21 February, and 6 March 1974).

changes, such as those involved in the consequences of changes in investment decisions or pricing practices and market structure, may become evident only after a period of several years.

Changes in cost allocation or accounting procedures designed to avoid the full impact of controls regulations and the need to develop specific information for review by stabilization authorities and supporting data for compliance auditing imposed costs that could be estimated by straightforward methods. Business practices that led to inefficient real resource usage in production and distribution imposed costs that are more difficult to measure. Purchasing policies designed to hedge against shortages, or disruption of smooth production flows when shortages were realized, imposed costs that are more obvious but not necessarily more important than the costs of inefficient patterns of input usage. The emergence of bartering arrangements as a substitute for transactions in the marketplace contributed to excessively large inventories, complicated marketing by increasing information and search costs necessary to assure timely delivery at the lowest available prices, and led to less efficient distribution than could be expected under uniform prices in the marketplace.

An example from ferrous scrap markets illustrates how controls can reduce efficiency. Steel scrap generated as a by-product of production operations for large firms was subject to price controls, but scrap collected from obsolete or worn-out items was not subject to price controls. Covering all of the junk dealers in the country was impractical, and higher prices in that market could stimulate increased scrap collection. Inefficiency in scrap distribution occurred when scrap subject to controls was sold through bartering arrangements in exchange for scarce items that it was used to produce, such as concrete reinforcement bars. In products produced from steel scrap, distribution inefficiencies occurred in response to wide differences in prices. These prices reflected differences in production costs which depended on the source and cost of the scrap input as well as on the fraction of scrap used in furnaces. Another reported business practice, for which costs imposed are more easily ascertainable, was transshipment of scrap from an industrial plant at one location to steelmaking facilities owned by the same company at another location to avoid sale of the scrap at controlled prices at one market location and purchases of a similar quantity at uncontrolled prices at another.[12]

[12] A brief discussion of price controls in the steel industry and a summary of actions that were taken to modify the regulations is contained in Appendix V of "Removing Controls: The Policy of Selective Decontrol," *Historical Working Papers on the Economic Stabilization Program*, 15 August 1971 to 30 April 1974, Part 2, pp. 942-47.

It was frequently alleged that controls were adversely affecting production levels, particularly when profit margin limits were an effective constraint. Evidence based on production levels attained is ambiguous, because the absolute limits on levels of production capability are usually impossible to define precisely for any firm or industry. Levels achieved depend in part on costs of marginal additions to output compared to prices realized in the market. In addition, firms operate in a dynamic and changing environment in which they must make decisions regarding small adjustments in the production process, expansion of some portion of production operations, or cutbacks in output by scaling down less efficient operations or close-down of obsolescent plants. Marginal changes in current production through such decisions over time could have a significant offsetting influence on price movements. Thus, it is possible that delays in price adjustments and price ceilings could attenuate production responses that would otherwise help to smooth adjustments in prices to changes in demand.

This discussion of controls and their costs can be summarized by brief consideration of two points. The first point is that the short-run costs of controls—at least as they were administered during the Economic Stabilization Program—were apparently not enormous. Evidence of adverse effects during the period of controls is generally not readily apparent in broad measures of production or other indicators either for individual industries or for the overall economy. Thus, in spite of widespread reports of shortages, inefficient business practices, and misallocation of resources, normal measures of economic activity for most sectors did not show pronounced adverse effects that can be directly traced to controls. The second point is that the costs of controls are nonetheless real, and they are not adequately captured by reference only to normal measures of production and economic activity. Resources are used to administer controls, with costs borne both by the government and the private sector. Symptoms of inefficiency that can obviously be traced to controls impose additional real costs, even though these costs are difficult to quantify. In addition, costs of a more subtle type are obscured by normal measures of economic activity, because the prices that are used in computing the value of economic output can be less closely identified with the value placed by society on measures of economic output as prices diverge more and more from market values.

6
CONTROLS AND RELATED POLICY ISSUES

Almost inevitably the success of controls as a stabilization tool will be judged by the public according to the inflation that occurs while they are in force. The influence of controls is frequently analyzed by economists to assess the extent to which actual prices diverged from the prices that would have occurred in the absence of controls. These analyses are necessarily based on assumptions concerning key variables—such as federal spending and the rate of monetary expansion—that might themselves have been influenced by the presence of controls. In addition, the divergence between projected and actual inflation has often in recent years been larger than could be attributed to incorrect assumptions about key variables. Both of these considerations—the effects of controls on key variables and the unexplained divergence between projected and actual inflation—dilute the confidence that can be placed in econometric estimates of the marginal influence of controls. Moreover, the potential marginal influence of controls on inflation depends on the extent to which their existence influences other economic policies, such as farm policy, and the degree to which policy objectives such as equity, efficiency, and availability of goods and materials are subordinated to short-run inflation concerns.

Whatever direct impact the controls regulations had on wages and prices, controls also influenced the context in which economic policy was made. To the extent that the controls temporarily suppressed price and wage increases, the full influence of market forces became evident to policy makers and the private sector only after some delay. To the extent that market pressures in specific sectors led to rapid price increases or dislocations under the controls, high-level attention was focused on possible policy changes that could influence supply or demand to relieve the pressures placed on controls by a market environment that was forcing prices up. Thus, the controls at times facilitated the development of specific policies that could help to reduce market pressures by shifting supply or demand—policies that were usually more complex but more promising than a simple limitation of short-run price or wage increases. Issues raised by this broad economic role of controls may be of more lasting importance than quantification of their direct effects on prices and wages in any period.

Controls and Demand Management

The possibility that the existence of a program of wage and price controls may have influenced the expansiveness of monetary and fiscal policy is of particular importance for evaluating the full influence of controls on inflation. Indeed, one of the thorniest issues in any attempt to assess the quantitative effects of controls is the issue of what components of economic policy should be treated as independent of controls. It is possible, for example, that controls were viewed as providing some short-run insurance against inflation, thereby shifting the balance toward accepting the risks of more expansionary policies than would have been planned in their absence. Controls may also have suppressed inflation sufficiently to mask for a time inflationary pressures building up in the economy, and consequently they may have delayed a recognition by policy makers that less expansionary policies were called for.

The effect that controls may have had on macroeconomic policy can be explored by examining some evidence concerning the period 1971–74. Even though no definitive conclusions can be drawn from them, official statements suggest that controls were regarded as providing a measure of protection against inflation, thereby permitting a more expansionary pattern of policies than would otherwise have been considered prudent.[1] The imposition of controls was also accompanied by requests for investment tax credits and tax reductions to stimulate the economy. In addition, the most widely used explanation of the manner in which controls were expected to help reduce inflation was that a major portion of the continuing inflation in 1971 could be attributed to the lingering effects of past inflation. The price and wage projections from standard models made it difficult to account for the rate at which inflation was occurring prior to controls on the

[1] *Economic Report of the President, 1972,* p. 69, pp. 101-102.

basis of demand conditions prevailing before the controls were imposed. The controls were viewed as reducing expectations of inflation by providing a period of lower inflation more consistent with the degree of slack in labor and product markets. Yet the risks of placing too much reliance on controls and moving toward overly expansive policies were also explicitly recognized and cautioned against.[2]

The extent to which inflation was actually suppressed by the controls (when measured against price levels that would have been sustained by competition in the marketplace) is uncertain. The limits that were placed on prices under controls, along with incentives to keep prices down voluntarily (either out of a spirit of cooperation or to avoid confrontation and possible audit for violations), inhibited market testing. Market signals were muted, and information on accumulating market pressures was received only after delays which added new uncertainty to government policy planning. This influence of controls was of uncertain importance during the period 1971 to 1974, but it may have delayed a turn toward more restrictive demand management policies.

Both monetary and fiscal policies were expansionary during the early phases of controls. These policies were generally viewed as appropriate for stimulating higher output and employment levels, particularly in the early stages of the recovery when fiscal policy was most expansionary. Federal deficits averaged $19 billion in 1971 and 1972, although the full employment deficit averaged only $5 billion, and small surpluses were achieved on both bases in 1973.[3] The net expansionary effect of tax and expenditure changes introduced with the New Economic Policy on the budget was estimated as $1.1 billion for fiscal year 1972,[4] a small impact compared to actual deficits at that time. Monetary policy remained expansionary during almost the entire period; the money supply increased at an average rate of about 7 percent, but the most rapid expansion took place in the latter part of 1972. Although in retrospect these policies seem to have been overly expansionary, particularly in the latter part of the period, the mistake appears to have resulted mainly from the deficiencies of economic forecasts rather than from policies that differed from those on which the forecasts were based. The upsurge in inflation that began in 1973 was not foreseen by professional forecasters.[5]

---

2 *Economic Report of the President, 1973,* p. 53, and *Economic Report of the President, 1972,* p. 96.

3 *Economic Report of the President, 1974,* p. 31.

4 *Economic Report of the President, 1972,* p. 71.

5 Appendix A of the *Statement of Dr. John T. Dunlop,* p. A-1.

Controls and Other Stabilization Policy Initiatives

The introduction of controls in the U.S. economy, and intermittently of incomes policies of various kinds in other countries, is less a tribute to their demonstrated durability and effectiveness than to the lack of constructive alternatives for responding to public pressures to "do something" that would have a visible and direct effect on inflation. It is appropriate that these pressures should converge on the government in democratic societies, and the government should give high priority to actions and policies that can help to contain inflation. Whether the imposition of generalized wage and price controls is the most constructive response in most instances, however, is open to question. It would be desirable to place more emphasis on the development of imaginative policies that would help to identify and attack the real economic problems of our society. Policy approaches that could help to increase supply, reduce costs, facilitate adjustment, or improve productivity would work more slowly and indirectly to reduce inflation, but such policies would also have less potential for simultaneously imposing costs through reduced efficiency and disappointing public expectations.

The establishment of a system of wage and price controls has, however, facilitated the formation of institutional structures for bringing together representatives of labor, business, the public sector, Congress, and the executive branch, in order to identify and discuss problems and explore possible approaches from different viewpoints. Since the cooperation, support, acquiescence, and expertise of each of these groups is necessary in varying degrees to the success of the effort (particularly the cooperation of organized labor), controls provide a framework for mobilizing public interest and attitudes and promoting serious exchange of views, statements of positions, and negotiation of compromise approaches. The Pay Board and advisory committees of Phase II, along with earlier exploratory meetings, the Construction Industry Stabilization Committee, and the Labor-Management Advisory Committee and tripartite committees in the food and health sectors during Phases III and IV provided some of the major forums for addressing broad policy issues and individual cases.

While the existence of a program of wage and price controls provided the immediate impetus for identifying and bringing together spokesmen representing various interests and involving them in the process of working toward solutions, controls may not have been a necessary precondition for establishing effective structures for policy discussions and problem solving. The Construction Industry Stabilization Committee (which could draw upon authority for direct controls before broader controls were imposed) and the Food Wage and Salary Committee (which could not do this after controls for most sectors were terminated) are examples of structures developed to deal with specific problem areas. It might be possible to establish similar structures in other instances, and these might contribute to the working out of industrial relations problems and the rationalization of wage patterns without authority for mandatory controls. Structures such as labor-management advisory committees set up to play a consultative and supportive role in the formation of national economic policy have often made modest but valuable contributions. The Conference on Inflation in September 1974 represents another approach to public dialogue on problems and issues. While controls have mobilized active participation and sometimes provided support for compromises by those representing relatively narrow interests to facilitate the achievement of broader goals, cooperation and participation in the resolution of many problems might often be elicited without the spur of comprehensive price and wage controls.

The stabilization program during the period from 1971 through 1974 also provided structures within the federal government for bringing together cabinet members responsive to different constituencies, a staff capability to identify for discussion policies that contributed to inflation, and a cabinet-level spokesman to focus attention on the inflationary implications of policy decisions. The main forum for internal policy review during Phase II was the Cost of Living Council itself, while the food and health policy committees were the most important forums during other phases of the program.

Controls, with their potential for market disruption, provided strong incentives to search for policy actions that could increase supply or restrain demand and thus reduce inflation. But the development of ways for the federal government to focus more attention on the inflationary consequences of government policy actions should not be dependent on controls. Controls on food prices are certainly not a necessary condition for systematic consideration of the potential impact on inflation of federal farm policy, an area in which federal government policy decisions are of major importance for production and prices. The Council on Wage and Price Stability, in some respects a successor to the Cost of Living Council, may contribute to the evolution of an internal governmental structure for discussion, review, and action on economic policy issues influencing inflation. The procedures for systematic budget review adopted by the Congress may also contribute to improved price stability.

The resurgence of inflation in 1973 gave new impetus to a search for ways in which productivity could be improved to relieve the pressure of rising costs on controls. Stabilization committees often provided a labor-management structure for the discussion of promising approaches and served as a catalyst for their implementation.[6] The rise toward capacity production levels, particularly in many of the basic materials producing and processing industries in early 1973, focused attention on the question of whether sufficient resources were being devoted to capital investment. Adequacy of capital investment and the contribution that additional new investment could make to improved productivity growth were two considerations that formed the background for the sectoral decontrol process during the last part of 1973 and early 1974. Adequacy of rates of return and willingness to make new investment commitments were factors considered in decontrol decisions. Securing capacity expansion commitments as controls were removed was part of an intricate process to facilitate orderly sectoral decontrol. Investment commitments provided a supporting rationale for sequential decontrol decisions, and they represented a significant effort to coordinate policies for achieving capacity expansion needs with policies for removing controls.[7]

Because the controls imposed limits and delays on price increases and because the regulations included limits on profit margins, investment decisions could have been adversely affected by controls. The influence that controls actually had on business investment, however, is not clear. Several factors suggest that their effects on reducing investment were small: the perceived short-term character of the controls, the influence of longer-term price and cost prospects on many investment decisions, the initial favorable attitude of the business community toward controls, and the apparently small impact of the controls on prices during 1972, particularly for industries producing basic materials where capacity limitations became most apparent in 1973. Other factors, however, suggest a larger effect: the full effect of prices in signaling increased profitability of investment was reduced to the extent that some prices were held below market levels, cash flow to finance increased investment was reduced, lower profitability impeded external financing, and incremental decisions to alter production operations or keep marginal production facilities in operation may have been affected. In the administration of controls,

[6] Such initiatives were facilitated by the fact that the director of the Cost of Living Council at that time also served as chairman of the Productivity Commission.

[7] See "Removing Controls: The Policy of Selective Decontrol" in *Historical Working Papers on the Economic Stabilization Program,* 15 August 1971 to 30 April 1974, Part 2, pp. 859-948, for a detailed discussion of the decontrol process.

policies regarding investment evolved from the maintenance of as neutral a policy as possible during the early stages of controls to the explicit encouragement of new investment in decontrol decisions. There was no apparent weakness in business investment during the controls period, a fact that may be attributed mainly to the "temporary" nature of the controls and to their initial favorable effect on public confidence.[8]

The flow of investment decisions in the economy plays a significant role in cyclical movements in demand. The investment tax credit introduced with the New Economic Policy was aimed at least as much toward stimulating demand as toward the need for providing increased productive capacity. Moreover, the capacity problem that emerged in 1973 was concentrated in the basic materials sector instead of being spread throughout the economy. These developments were apparently not foreseen by the firms in the industries concerned, and they were only belatedly recognized by the government. Improved forecasts of capacity needs could have helped to reduce inflation from this source as well as to smooth investment flow and its impact on aggregate demand. Better information on actual production capacity could contribute to more informed assessments of capacity needs. The influence of safety and environmental legislation on the relation between total investment and additions to actual physical output capacity has also increased in recent years. (Capital expenditures made for pollution control do not increase capacity.) Moreover, in developing projections of potential output to guide short-run demand management policies, measures of industrial production capacity may be as important as measures of employment conditions. While there is little reason to assume that capacity needs for particular industries could be foreseen any more accurately by a government agency than by firms and investors in the private sector, more detailed and carefully assembled information might contribute to an improved assessment of intentions and prospects by both the government and private sectors.

Controls and the Public

When inflation becomes an issue of public concern, price increases for particular products come to be looked at mainly from the point of

[8] Some evidence of a possible small favorable influence on investment during the controls period is contained in Roland G. Droitsch, "The Impact of the Economic Stabilization Program on Business Fixed Investment," *Historical Working Papers on the Economic Stabilization Program*, Part 2, pp. 949-988.

view of their contribution to inflation instead of from the point of view of their role in allocating resources in response to reduced supply or increased demand. The existence of formal controls provides a channel for responding to public and political pressures to deal with particular price increases. The temptation is strong to apply rigid controls to specific products, to set limits on the size of individual price increases, or to apply tight rules for sectors in which increased stringency can make no contribution to the real problem. For example, the policy response to the fact that lumber prices were rising more rapidly than most other prices in 1972 was to apply more stringent controls, when decontrol might have made a greater contribution toward the underlying problem of supply. Restraining prices in sectors where demand pressures could not be accommodated through short-term supply increases was generally inconsistent with the broad approach of Phase II, but it was as awkward politically to exempt lumber prices then as it was easy to exempt them in 1973 when lumber prices were falling.

The retention of mandatory controls on food prices for Phase III provides an example of controls policy oriented more toward the presumed adverse political reaction to voluntary, self-administered controls on food prices when food prices were expected to rise significantly than toward the economic contribution that continued mandatory controls on food prices could be expected to make. The public impact of retention of mandatory controls on food prices was apparently small, because the public was not persuaded by statements explaining how the surge in food prices could not be attributed to the shift to Phase III in view of continued mandatory controls on food prices. Until ceiling prices were imposed for meat, the continuing mandatory controls on food prices were structured to permit pass-through of costs, and they had little disruptive effect on markets because they permitted large price increases. The meat ceilings were addressed in part to another goal—preservation of wage/cost stability—and their influence on wage trends should be weighed against whatever costs they imposed on the economy. Continued mandatory controls on food prices may also have assisted the government in managing its internal policy decisions to increase supply. They may also have increased the acceptability of these policy changes to some segments of the food industry.

The shift in public attitudes reflected by congressional debate and action between the first half of 1973 and the last half of 1973 through early 1974 leads one to ask whether the political process will permit implementation of controls in a manner seeking to avoid distortions and inefficiency in the economy.[9] A significant shift in public attitudes toward the merit of stringent controls did not occur until after the graphic illustrations of market disruptions and adverse effects on supply that occurred during the freeze beginning in June 1973. These demonstrations of the futility of stringent controls under the conditions prevailing then and the shortages that emerged later in the year apparently led to increased recognition that stringent controls could be counterproductive.

Limitations of Controls

One of the most fundamental but often misunderstood features of controls is the limited potential they have for contributing to lower inflation—that is, lower inflation than would have occurred in their absence and without the adverse side effects that most of their proponents would prefer to avoid. Under emergency conditions (such as a major war effort) the scale of the diversion of resources that must be accomplished is sufficiently large that major strains are inevitable, and the inefficiency and inequity of controls and rationing may be more tolerable than other methods of securing the necessary adjustments. The goals of peacetime incomes policies in Western industrial societies, however, have been much more limited than containment of the inflationary effects of wartime resource diversion. Direct controls on prices and wages to effect the goals of incomes policies have usually been viewed as a supplement to reliance on pricing in the marketplace, although admittedly in some economies they have been viewed as an essential supplement. Draconian systems of controls have generally been avoided, except for short periods, both because their effects are not tolerated for long by the major participants in the economy and because the costs they impose on the economy exceed any benefits that might be achieved through lower inflation.

The manner in which controls are expected to affect the process of inflation is usually not carefully articulated in discussions of the possible contribution of incomes policies. In some instances reference

[9] Most of the significant legislative initiatives in Congress before mid-1973 were intended to tighten controls. After mid-1973 most were intended to relieve the pinch of controls; many bills and resolutions to end controls were introduced, and several resolutions or bills were introduced to provide relief from controls in sectors such as food, fertilizer, petrochemicals and steel. See the listing of legislative activities from 1 May 1973 to 30 April 1974 in Appendix C of "Congress and Controls," *Historical Working Papers on the Economic Stabilization Program*, Part 1, pp. 220-243.

is made to market power and to a range of discretion that may exist in establishing administered prices or negotiating wage increases for large economic units.[10] Of course, the existing structure of markets falls short of fully competitive conditions and results in price and wage relationships that depart from those that would prevail under fully competitive conditions. If controls are aimed primarily at offsetting these departures from fully competitive price and wage relationships, their limited influence over inflation and the strains they would be confronted with should be viewed in perspective. For example, if profits for 20 percent of the private nonfarm business sector (and 20 percent represents a generous estimate of the proportion that would be described by some as characterized by "administered" prices) had been held at their 1970 cyclical low until 1972, only six-tenths of a percentage point would have been shaved from the cumulative increase in prices during the two-year period in which profits in that sector rose by 20 percent. Aiming controls toward offsetting noncompetitive wage/price relationships would compel explicit attention to the question of whether rates of return were adequate to support investment and maintenance of production capacity in the sectors affected. A one-time reduction in prices and rates of return of this kind would, of course, make no continuing contribution to reduced inflation. This estimate, of course, assumes no changes in other factors, and it does not adequately reflect the possible influence of such a policy on the dynamics of price changes. In any case, the short-run dynamics of inflation are not well understood, so the full influence of such a policy would be difficult to predict.

The possible contribution of controls in effectively reducing relative wages in some of the more highly organized, high-wage sectors of the economy is more difficult to assess because wage structural linkages extend well beyond the employee units that might be placed in this category. If wage increases of 10 percent of the private nonfarm work force were depressed to one-half of the average rate of wage increase during two years of the controls, the direct effect on private nonfarm prices would have been only four-tenths of a percentage point on prices, although the impact through indirect effects on other wages could be quite large. Yet such a policy could be maintained only until the influence on relative wages of labor market power was offset, and there would be no further continuing influence on the rate of inflation. An approach designed to alter relative wage relationships under controls would obviously need to

[10] *Economic Report of the President, 1962,* p. 185.

be much more subtle than is suggested by the arithmetic describing its potential direct impact. Even if a realignment of relative wage positions could be achieved by use of controls, the forces that generated the prevailing patterns are undoubtedly strong and would pose a continuing threat of labor strife to re-establish the previous wage differentials.

Except for very short periods, the impact on prices of restricting pass-through of increased costs and squeezing corporate profits is much smaller than seems to be generally recognized. The cumulative rise in prices attributable to inflation within the corporate nonfinancial sector between the beginning of 1971 and the end of 1973 was 8.7 percent. If profit margins had been held to their low cyclical position at the beginning of the period, the rise in prices would have been reduced by less than one percentage point.

Incomes policies could also be developed that are not oriented toward restructuring broad relative price or wage relationships. These policies could be directed toward a roughly parallel reduction in inflation across all sectors. The controls of 1971–74, for example, were initially designed to limit price adjustments throughout the economy to the magnitude of short-term cost increases and to influence the size of cost increases primarily by establishing a standard to reduce the size of wage increases. This was viewed as an approach that would help achieve an actual reduction in inflation during a period in which generalized excess demand was not an immediate threat. Revision of expectations and the development of contracts and practices reflecting lower rates of inflation were expected to exercise a stabilizing influence, similar in kind but opposite in direction to the influence that was attributed to the buildup of inflation in the late 1960s on price increases in 1970 and 1971.

Price developments in 1973, particularly the surge in food prices and the large increases in basic materials prices and petroleum prices later in the year, created a vastly different economic environment from what had been projected. These price developments should not necessarily be regarded as a challenge to the validity of the concepts on which the controls were initially based, nor should they necessarily be regarded as a demonstration of the inappropriateness of the limited purposes of the controls under the conditions that were projected in 1971. Instead they serve as a reminder of the crucial importance for short-term price performance of market developments in a limited number of critical sectors, such as food and energy. More generally, they serve as a reminder of the flexibility of the price system as a mechanism for promoting rapid adjustments to change in the marketplace. The price surge that began in 1973 also indicated that, whatever contribution controls may have made during 1972, they could have little marginal influence under the conditions that emerged in 1973 unless controls policy was shifted toward establishing rigid ceilings and supplementing the ceilings with subsidies and nonprice rationing mechanisms as necessary—which would of course have been a policy with an entirely different conceptual basis.

Controls may in some instances make a limited contribution toward facilitating adjustment to lower inflation when no large shifts in supply or demand are projected. Such a contribution could be made by altering public expectations of inflation, for example, if inflationary expectations are an important source of momentum in price and wage increases. Controls are vulnerable to serious failure, however, by neither containing inflation nor avoiding potentially costly inefficiency when major supply or demand shifts occur. The normal function of the market system, of course, is to generate automatic adjustments of prices and consumption to changes in market conditions—changes that are constantly occurring and usually not accurately foreseen. This raises the question of whether the costs that controls may impose before they can be gracefully terminated, or over time if continued indefinitely, may exceed the benefits of whatever limited contribution they may make.

7
SUMMARY AND CONCLUSIONS

Economic stabilization policy in the period 1971–74 was shaped by both economic considerations and political forces. Controls on wages and prices were reluctantly imposed by the administration in August 1971 as an anti-inflation initiative to complement other policy actions, since the policies that were introduced to stimulate expansion in aggregate demand and to deal with the international payments imbalance would both tend to raise inflation. The threat of an international financial crisis—the economic problem with most immediacy—was addressed by suspension of the convertibility of the dollar into gold. Public concern about the level of unemployment and rising public support for direct intervention in wage-price policy provided the major impetus for the expansionary fiscal policy proposals and the price and wage controls. It was recognized that controls could contribute to slower inflation by reducing inflationary expectations and by helping to ensure that wage and price inflation would in fact subside in line with several favorable factors in the outlook. The decision to impose controls was based on a judgment that the program could be a constructive response to public pressures for an "incomes policy," but this judgment was tempered with a recognition that the effectiveness and durability of controls would reflect their limitations as an economic stabilization tool.

The Phase II controls of 1972 were designed and administered to contribute as effectively as possible to achieving lower inflation, but a strong emphasis was also placed on minimizing bureaucratic intervention in particular wage and price decisions and on avoiding adverse side effects such as market disruption, distortions, or shortages. Moreover, the controls were intended from the outset to be a short-term policy tool and not a permanent institutional structure to alter the price and wage setting process. The shift to Phase III in 1973 as a step toward gradual removal of controls failed to achieve that objective, however, because a new surge in inflation began that brought with it increasing pressure to reinstate tougher controls.

The June 1973 freeze followed by Phase IV represented a temporary reversal in the direction of controls policies. Recourse to the freeze and to mandatory controls was largely a policy response to the widespread public perception that the resurgence of price inflation was to an important extent attributable to the termination of Phase II and the changes in the administration of the controls that were introduced at that time. These public attitudes were reflected by initiatives in the Congress threatening drastically more rigid and stringent controls, and the freeze was imposed in reaction to these developments. During the freeze and the stringent controls that followed, it became increasingly recognized by the public that controls could not prevent a rise in inflation without causing serious market disruption and adverse effects on supply. This gradual shift in public attitudes contributed to public acceptance of gradual, selective decontrol in late 1973 and early 1974 in spite of the rise in inflation to rates above 10 percent.

During 1972, the policy approach designed to minimize market disruption, shortages, and other unfavorable side effects of price and wage controls had been consistent with achieving reduced inflation. In 1973, however, when the market environment became unfavorable, a rise in inflation could not be averted by the move to controls more stringent than those of Phase II, in spite of a policy approach in administering the controls in which relief was not generally granted unless potentially serious market disruptions or shortages were in prospect. Administration of the controls with a sensitivity to avoiding serious distortion of relative prices, shortages, and other adverse side effects was desirable on economic grounds, but public pressures and congressional initiatives to relieve the pinch of controls in the second half of 1973 provide a strong indication that a less sensitive policy approach would also have failed to receive political acceptance.

The limits on stringency in administering the controls that were set by the political context and by economic goals other than short-term containment of inflation meant that the controls could be expected to have only a marginal influence on price performance. The data on construction wages and health care costs support a conclusion that controls significantly reduced inflation in those sectors in both 1972 and 1973. In 1972, they temporarily suppressed inflation in some other sectors such as lumber, and they may have contributed marginally to lower inflation throughout the economy by dampening inflationary expectations and moderating wage increases. In addition, controls may have helped to ensure that actual price and wage developments in 1972 were within the range that could be expected on the basis of factors such as improved balance in the wage structure and a cyclical rise in productivity growth—factors which also contributed heavily to the appearance of success that was achieved by the Phase II controls.

In 1973 a marked change in the market environment brought about conditions in which rising price inflation could not be contained by controls without serious adverse side effects. The major factors were strong domestic demand supported by high monetary expansion rates in 1972, the decline in world food supply, strong cyclical demand in international markets, the decline in the foreign exchange value of the dollar, pressures on production capacity in many basic materials industries, and, late in 1973, the oil embargo and the massive rise in oil prices put into effect by the cartel of major oil-exporting countries. With the rise in inflation the controls appeared unsuccessful, and since the rise in inflation coincided closely with the shift to Phase III, the Phase III controls were widely regarded as ineffective.

Public and political attention was focused primarily on the apparent ineffectiveness of Phase III controls, perhaps partly because the changes in market conditions in 1973 and their implications for prices were not foreseen or initially fully recognized even by those forecasting or interpreting economic trends. However, the changes that were occurring in the marketplace during 1973 made it impossible to contain inflation within a range comparable with that experienced during Phase II without controls that were based on a radically different and more stringent approach in which other economic goals were very heavily subordinated to short-term inflation control. Analysis of data on prices, costs, productivity and profits indicates that the rise in inflation in 1973 occurred as a result of changes in underlying economic factors, and not as a result of business pricing practices that violated the stabilization regulations and pricing concepts that had been applied since the beginning of the program. Because the rise in inflation in 1973 resulted from changes in the market environment and not from a breakdown in cooperation and compliance with the stabilization regulations, continuation of the Phase II controls could have done little to moderate inflation in early 1973. For the same reasons, the shift to more rigid and stringent controls in the second half of the year was accompanied by continued high inflation in spite of the rising incidence of shortages and distortions which reflected prices held below market clearing levels.

Indications that controls were keeping prices below levels they would have reached in the absence of controls were more prevalent in late 1973 than they had been in 1972. Evidence that prices were held below market clearing levels in late 1973 included widespread reports of shortages, black markets or "gray" markets, and difficulties in obtaining supplies and materials. Whatever marginal influence on prices the controls may have had in 1973, however, was dwarfed by the faster pace at which prices were rising.

Administering a system of wage and price controls involves making decisions on particular prices and wage situations. Circumstances surrounding particular wage situations are usually viewed by the parties to the wage adjustment as being sufficiently unique so that they cannot be satisfactorily dealt with by even a fairly complex system of rules and procedures, but are instead properly the subject for bargaining and negotiation. Market pressures for price increases or requests for increases in particular prices by individual firms must be dealt with in the context of cost conditions, market demand, and other applicable factors. Only a fraction of the information that was available to those intimately familiar with their firms or industries, and which would be reflected by pricing in the marketplace, could be assembled to guide decisions on particular prices by those administering the controls. The information that could be assembled for particular cases often brought into sharp focus the dilemma of choosing between either a rise in price or the threat of shortages, distortions, or adverse effects on supply or investment. Particularly during 1973, analysis of specific price situations revealed few instances in which any appreciable effect on prices could be obtained by limiting or delaying increases without a strong potential for disrupting markets, impairing efficiency, or reducing supply.

The acceleration of inflation that began in late 1972 and early 1973 stimulated an emphasis on and search for policies that could improve the market environment for controls by relieving pressures that were causing prices to rise. The potential for adverse side effects that would result from attempts to contain inflation instead by more stringent controls may have contributed to this emphasis. A wide range of actions was taken to increase supply including removal of beef import restrictions, expansion of timber supply from the national forests, and sales of stock-piled materials. The most significant of these actions aimed at relieving market pressures by increasing supply was in the area of federal farm policy, where the major liberalization that occurred in late 1972 and early 1973 may have been facilitated by the presence of controls. While these policies were not sufficient to prevent a major surge in inflation in 1973 and 1974, they kept the surge smaller than what might otherwise have occurred during that period.

The full effects of the controls during the period 1971–74 are not easily measured. Analysis of their effects is complicated by the fact that controls displaced the path of inflation over time and indirectly influenced other policies. The marginal effects of controls on inflation while they were in force cannot be measured with any precision, because little confidence can be placed in the accuracy of estimates of the course inflation might have taken if there had been no program of wage and price controls. Among the sectors in which controls seem to have deflected inflation trends, however, the most significant were construction wages, health care costs, and since 1973, petroleum product prices. The controls, of course, temporarily suppressed wage and price increases in several other sectors. The most durable impact on restraining inflation through controls probably occurred through their influence on construction wage increases, although some lasting moderating influence on wages may also have occurred more generally in other sectors in which restraint was accompanied by improved balance in the wage structure or more constructive industrial relations practices.

Both economic considerations and political factors placed limits on the aggressiveness and stringency with which wage and price controls policies could be administered by the government. Even during a period in which inflation was clearly an issue of serious concern, public opinion and congressional attitudes also appropriately reflected concern for other economic and social goals, particularly when adverse effects of controls became evident. Concerns other than short-term price inflation included the avoidance of serious market disruption and reduced efficiency, preservation of institutional arrangements such as collective bargaining and markets in which the interplay of supply and demand largely determine price, production and investment decisions, and maintenance of the freedom in private decision making that these institutional arrangements permit. In this context only a small, and usually temporary, influence on inflation could be expected in most sectors through controls. This review of experience during the period 1971–74 indicates that a more significant impact on inflation by controls that place limits on wage and price increases could only have been achieved if there had been a more pronounced subordination of other important goals than was considered acceptable under the Economic Stabilization Program.

APPENDIX

List of Appendix Tables

List of Appendix Figures

Table A-1

PERCENTAGE INCREASES IN HOURLY EARNINGS AND NEGOTIATED WAGE RATE INCREASES IN MAJOR COLLECTIVE BARGAINING SETTLEMENTS, 1968–73

	1968	1969	1970	1971	1972	1973
Average hourly earnings,[a] private nonfarm	6.6	6.6	6.7	7.0	6.3	6.2
Wage rate increases under collective bargaining agreements[b]						
All industries						
First year	7.4	9.2	11.9	11.6	7.3	5.8
Deferred	4.6	5.4	5.8	7.7	6.0	4.8
Construction						
First year	8.7	13.1	17.6	12.6	6.9	5.0
Deferred	n.a.	n.a.	10.1	13.1	11.6	7.3
Manufacturing						
First year	7.0	7.9	8.1	10.9	6.6	5.9
Deferred	3.9	4.0	4.6	4.8	4.5	4.4
Nonmanufacturing (excluding construction)						
First year	7.6	9.6	14.2	12.2	7.5	6.0
Deferred	n.a.	n.a.	5.2	7.6	7.3	5.0

[a] Adjusted for overtime (in manufacturing only) and interindustry employment shifts.

[b] Limited to private settlements covering 1,000 workers or more. Data for 1973 are preliminary. Comparable data for years prior to 1968 are not available.

Source: U.S. Department of Labor, Bureau of Labor Statistics.

Table A–2

EFFECTIVE WAGE ADJUSTMENTS IN MANUFACTURING
(median changes, percent)

Year	All Union	Nonunion	Union/Nonunion Difference
1961	2.7	1.0	+1.7
1962	2.6	1.6	+1.0
1963	2.6	2.8	−0.2
1964	2.2	2.0	+0.2
1965	2.9	3.2	−0.3
1966	3.2	3.9	−0.7
1967	4.0	4.6	−0.6
1968	5.0	5.0	0.0
1969	5.0	5.1	−0.1
1970	5.7	5.1	+0.6
1971	6.1	4.7	+1.4
1972	5.2	5.0	+0.2
	Average Annual Effective Wage Adjustments		
1961–64	2.5	1.8	+0.7
1965–69	4.0	4.4	−0.4
1970–72	5.7	4.9	+0.8

Note: Effective adjustments include cost of living adjustments, new increases, deferred increases, and decreases or no-change situations.

Source: U.S. Department of Labor, Bureau of Labor Statistics.

Table A-3

PROFITS AND PROFIT MARGINS FOR SELECTED INDUSTRIES: ANNUAL AND CUMULATIVE CHANGES, 1971–73

($ billions at annual rates)

		Calculated Increments to Profits		
	Change in Corporate Profits (1)	To maintain constant percentage margin (2)	Change in percentage profit margin (3)	Difference between constant percentage and constant dollar profit margin (4)
ANNUAL				
All industries				
1971	13.5	12.6	.9	7.4
1972	19.7	16.8	2.9	6.2
1973	35.2	22.7	12.5	11.4
Manufacturing				
1971	4.3	1.0	3.3	.4
1972	8.4	2.9	5.5	.1
1973	5.2	4.4	.8	.4
Agriculture				
1971	1.0	1.0	0.0	.1
1972	3.3	2.1	1.2	2.3
1973	19.1	10.5	8.6	9.5
Wholesale and retail trade				
1971	2.9	2.4	.5	1.4
1972	1.8	2.5	−.7	.4
1973	2.8	3.1	−.3	2.0
CUMULATIVE[a]				
All industries				
1972	19.7	16.8	2.9	6.2
1973	54.9	39.1	15.8	17.7
Manufacturing				
1972	8.4	2.9	5.5	.1
1973	13.6	6.7	6.9	.5
Agriculture				
1972	3.3	2.1	1.2	2.3
1973	22.4	12.0	10.4	11.3
Wholesale and retail trade				
1972	1.8	2.5	−.7	.4
1973	4.6	5.7	−1.1	2.5

Note: Profits figures refer to profit type income, which consists of corporate profits including inventory valuation adjustment, proprietors' income, rental income of persons, and surplus of government enterprises less subsidies. Output is measured in terms of value added as reported in the national income accounts.

[a] Annual changes may not sum to cumulative totals because of rounding and cumulative totals for components may differ in addition because they are cumulated on the basis of the percentage margin prevailing in 1971.

Source: U.S. Department of Commerce, Bureau of Economic Analysis.

Table A-4

PRICES AND THEIR RELATION TO PROFITS FOR SELECTED INDUSTRIES: ANNUAL AND CUMULATIVE INCREMENTS, 1971–73

	Change in Implicit Price Deflator (1)	**Calculated Increments to Price Change** Change in percentage profit margin (2)	Difference between constant percentage and constant dollar profit margin (3)
ANNUAL			
All industries			
1971	4.6	.1	.7
1972	3.3	.3	.5
1973	5.6	1.0	.9
Manufacturing			
1971	1.7	1.3	.2
1972	.4	1.9	0.0
1973	.9	.3	.1
Agriculture			
1971	.7	.1	.4
1972	15.2	3.5	6.9
1973	48.4	21.2	23.4
Wholesale and retail trade			
1971	5.5	.3	.8
1972	1.3	−.4	.2
1973	6.6	−.1	1.0
CUMULATIVE[a]			
All industries			
1972	3.3	.3	.5
1973	9.1	1.3	1.5
Manufacturing			
1972	.4	1.9	0.0
1973	1.4	2.2	0.1
Agriculture			
1972	15.2	3.5	6.9
1973	71.0	29.6	32.2
Wholesale and retail trade			
1972	1.3	−.4	.2
1973	8.0	−.5	1.2

[a] Annual changes may not sum to cumulative totals because of rounding, and cumulative totals for components may differ in addition because they are cumulated on the basis of the percentage margin prevailing in 1971.

Source: U.S. Department of Commerce, Bureau of Economic Analysis.

Table A–5

OUTPUT PER MAN-HOUR CHANGES AND PROFIT MARGINS IN MANUFACTURING: ANNUAL AND CUMULATIVE CHANGES, 1971–73

	Annual Percentage Change in Output per Man-hour (1)	Difference between Trend Rate and Short-Term Output per Man-hour Change[a] (2)	Calculated Increments to Profits ($ billions at annual rate)	
			Difference in rates of output per man-hour change[b] (3)	Change in percentage profit margin (4)
Annual				
1971	6.8	3.4	6.4	3.3
1972	6.4	3.0	6.3	5.4
1973	5.9	2.6	6.0	.8
Cumulative[c]				
1972	6.4	3.0	6.3	5.4
1973	12.4	5.6	12.4	6.9

[a] The trend rate of increase in output per man-hour was calculated as the compound annual rate of increase from 1958 through 1969, the period used by the Price Commission for developing rates of productivity growth for use as offsets to wage cost increases. The trend rate for the manufacturing sector was a 3.4 percent annual rate.

[b] Increments to profits and prices attributed to the difference between short-term and trend rates of change in output per man-hour are calculated by applying the differential in output per man-hour changes to the compensation share of value added in the manufacturing sector.

[c] Annual changes may not sum to cumulative totals because of rounding and cumulative totals for components may differ in addition because they are cumulated on the basis of the percentage margin prevailing in 1971.

Source: U.S. Department of Commerce, Bureau of Economic Analysis.

Table A–6

U.S. EXPORTS OF PORK TO MAJOR MARKETS, BY MONTHS, 1972–74

(millions of pounds)

	Jan.	Feb.	March	April	May	June	July	Aug.	Sept.	Oct.	Nov.	Dec.	Total
Canada													
1972	.9	1.1	1.8	2.7	1.8	2.0	2.1	2.7	4.2	5.4	3.7	3.1	31.6
1973	3.5	5.2	6.3	3.2	3.4	2.0	1.9	.7	3.6	7.1	4.0	2.5	43.4
1974	2.1	1.0	.8	2.2	3.2	5.4	4.0	5.4	8.6	7.5	5.8	5.0	51.0
Caribbean													
1972	.9	1.0	.4	1.1	1.1	1.0	1.0	.6	.7	1.3	1.6	1.5	12.8
1973	.9	.9	1.0	.9	1.3	1.1	1.0	1.0	.8	1.2	2.1	.8	12.9
1974	.9	.7	1.0	1.0	.8	.9	.9	.9	1.0	1.1	1.6	1.5	12.3
Japan													
1972	.1	.2	1.0	5.3	15.0	9.6	2.3	.8	2.2	9.4	.4	.8	46.3
1973	.6	5.1	24.3	25.1	23.4	9.4	1.9	1.1	.9	4.1	.6	.5	96.8
1974	.5	.2	.8	.8	.8	1.1	1.1	5.3	4.3	5.6	.8	.2	21.5
Others													
1972	.8	.8	.6	.8	.7	.5	.6	.7	.7	.7	.8	.9	8.6
1973	.3	.4	.6	.6	.6	1.2	.4	.6	.3	.7	1.0	.8	7.6
1974	.6	.5	.7	.9	.7	.9	1.2	.7	.8	.9	1.2	.8	9.9
Totals													
1972	2.7	3.1	3.8	9.9	18.5	13.1	6.0	4.8	7.8	16.8	6.5	6.3	99.3
1973	5.3	11.6	32.2	29.8	28.7	13.7	5.2	3.4	5.6	13.1	7.7	4.6	160.7
1974	4.1	2.4	3.3	4.9	5.4	8.3	7.1	12.4	14.8	15.1	9.4	7.5	94.7

Source: U.S. Department of Agriculture, Foreign Agricultural Service.

Table A–7

U.S. EXPORTS OF LIVE CATTLE TO CANADA, BY MONTHS, 1971–74

(number of head)

Month	1971	1972	1973	1974
January	30,799	3,540	2,494	7,190
February	4,004	391	1,520	18,222
March	4,082	3,378	2,994	20,381
April	4,171	11,456	1,634	2,488
May	1,477	8,320	2,480	405
June	2,778	2,688	3,710	416
July	1,291	1,133	4,430	145
August	257	714	17,071	128
September	157	527	39,124	7,988
October	379	334	64,204	11,524
November	1,165	17,358	27,306	8,203
December	7,398	11,520	18,351	12,237
Total	57,958	61,359	185,318	89,327

[a] Estimated.

Note: Cattle exports include all cattle except breeding cattle.

Source: U.S. Department of Agriculture, Foreign Agricultural Service.

Table A–8

U.S. IMPORTS OF BEEF AND PORK FROM CANADA

(1,000 pounds)

	Jan.	Feb.	Mar.	Apr.	May	June	July	Aug.	Sept.	Oct.	Nov.	Dec.	Total
Beef													
1972	4,133	3,992	4,121	4,738	6,145	6,436	5,749	5,573	4,557	4,387	4,802	3,663	58,298
1973	3,381	3,436	3,384	4,185	5,643	4,445	4,578	14,072	5,649	2,746	2,235	2,550	56,304
1974	3,818	5,094	3,260	2,096	2,638	2,347	2,643	3,114	2,884	2,889	4,215	1,912	36,910
Pork													
1972	7,008	7,067	6,958	5,566	6,342	6,400	6,440	5,611	3,848	4,062	4,636	3,596	67,532
1973	4,043	4,533	5,158	6,213	6,872	7,425	6,365	9,747	5,387	3,929	4,855	3,711	68,238
1974	6,485	7,317	5,719	3,321	4,010	3,238	3,696	3,887	3,608	3,834	5,569	3,028	53,712

Source: U.S. Department of Agriculture, Foreign Agricultural Service.

Table A–9

MEAT PRICE SPECIALS AS MEASURED BY PRICE AND VOLUME EFFECTS, 1971–74

(cents per pound)

Year/ Month	Beef	Pork	Year/ Month	Beef	Pork
1971			*1973*		
Jan.	6.1	6.2	Jan.	3.8	2.9
Feb.	4.1	6.2	Feb.	3.8	4.3
March	4.8	5.3	March	3.5	3.6
April	3.5	6.1	April	4.0	4.6
May	4.8	6.5	May	3.6	4.3
June	4.6	5.3	June	4.0	3.3
July	5.8	4.4	July	3.6	2.1
Aug.	5.3	4.4	Aug.	0.3	2.0
Sept.	4.8	5.2	Sept.	2.3	3.3
Oct.	5.4	4.9	Oct.	5.3	4.9
Nov.	4.1	4.4	Nov.	5.3	5.5
Dec.	2.8	3.8	Dec.	5.0	4.1
1972			*1974*		
Jan.	3.6	3.2	Jan.	3.8	4.6
Feb.	3.3	3.3	Feb.	4.5	5.0
March	4.0	5.6	March	6.4	6.1
April	5.4	5.2	April	5.8	6.8
May	5.4	4.4	May	5.4	6.1
June	4.3	3.0	June	6.1	5.8
July	3.6	3.2	July	4.8	4.0
Aug.	4.3	2.9	Aug.	5.6	3.8
Sept.	6.1	2.9	Sept.	6.6	4.6
Oct.	5.4	3.0	Oct.	8.2	4.9
Nov.	5.6	3.8	Nov.	8.2	4.9
Dec.	4.8	3.8	Dec.	8.4	5.5

Source: U.S. Department of Agriculture, Economic Research Service, Commodity Economics Division.

Table A–10

SOFTWOOD LUMBER PRODUCTION, NET TRADE AND STOCKS, 1971–74

(billions of board feet)

Year/ Month	Softwood Production[a]	Net Imports[b]	Stocks[c]
1971	29.7	6.5	4.3
January	2.2	.4	4.9
February	2.4	.4	4.8
March	2.8	.6	4.8
April	2.9	.5	4.7
May	2.6	.6	4.7
June	2.8	.7	4.5
July	2.6	.7	4.5
August	2.7	.5	4.4
September	2.7	.7	4.4
October	2.6	.4	4.3
November	2.5	.5	4.3
December	2.4	.6	4.3
1972	31.4	8.0	3.6
January	2.4	.7	4.3
February	2.6	.6	4.3
March	2.9	.6	4.2
April	2.7	.6	4.1
May	2.9	.8	3.9
June	2.8	.6	3.8
July	2.6	.7	3.7
August	2.8	.6	3.7
September	2.7	.7	3.7
October	2.9	.7	3.7
November	2.6	.8	3.7
December	2.2	.6	3.6
1973	31.6	7.6	3.9
January	2.5	.8	3.6
February	2.5	.6	3.6
March	2.9	.7	3.7
April	2.8	.6	3.7
May	2.8	.7	3.7
June	2.7	.7	3.6
July	2.5	.7	3.6
August	2.8	.4	3.6
September	2.6	1.2	3.7
October	2.8	.6	3.8
November	2.5	.5	3.8
December	2.2	.5	4.0

Table A–10 *(continued)*

SOFTWOOD LUMBER PRODUCTION, NET TRADE AND STOCKS, 1971–74

(billions of board feet)

Year/ Month	Softwood Production[a]	Net Imports[b]	Stocks[c]
1974	28.0	5.6	4.3
January	2.3	.5	4.1
February	2.4	.4	4.2
March	2.7	.5	4.1
April	2.9	.5	4.2
May	2.7	.6	4.1
June	2.4	.6	4.2
July	2.3	.5	4.3
August	2.4	.4	4.4
September	2.2	.5	4.5
October	2.2	.4	4.5
November	1.7	.3	4.4
December	1.5	.3	4.3

[a] National forest products.

[b] Total sawmill products.

[c] Gross mill end.

Source: U.S. Department of Commerce, Bureau of Economic Analysis, *Business Statistics 1973* (Washington, D. C.: U.S. Government Printing Office, 1973), p. 148, and Monthly *Survey of Current Business*, S-31.

Table A–11

CATTLE HIDE PRICES AND EXPORTS, 1971–74

Month	Prices for Light Native Steer Hides (cents per pound)				Exports (millions of hides)			
	1971	1972	1973	1974	1971	1972	1973	1974
January	15.38	20.33	45.40	37.93	1.2	1.3	1.5	1.4
February	15.84	21.49	44.55	37.94	1.3	1.2	1.8	1.5
March	15.90	25.68	40.20	32.76	1.6	1.7	1.8	1.5
April	17.00	28.85	35.85	31.68	1.2	1.1	1.3	1.6
May	16.68	30.03	36.31	30.76	1.3	1.4	1.4	1.6
June	15.86	31.07	35.49	27.84	1.2	1.2	1.3	1.1
July	15.33	32.18	36.07	26.43	.7	2.1	1.2	1.6
August	15.47	33.65	39.89	24.10	1.2	1.3	1.1	1.5
September	15.81	36.83	35.74	25.58	1.3	1.2	1.2	1.4
October	16.04	44.65	35.48	21.29	1.6	1.9	1.5	1.6
November	17.16	46.21	35.55	20.47	1.7	1.7	1.4	1.7
December	18.38	43.63	36.25	20.00	1.7	1.5	1.4	1.9

Source: U.S. Department of Commerce.

Figure A–1

CHANGES IN PRICES AND UNIT LABOR COSTS AND DIFFERENCE IN CHANGES FOR NONFINANCIAL CORPORATIONS, 1959–73

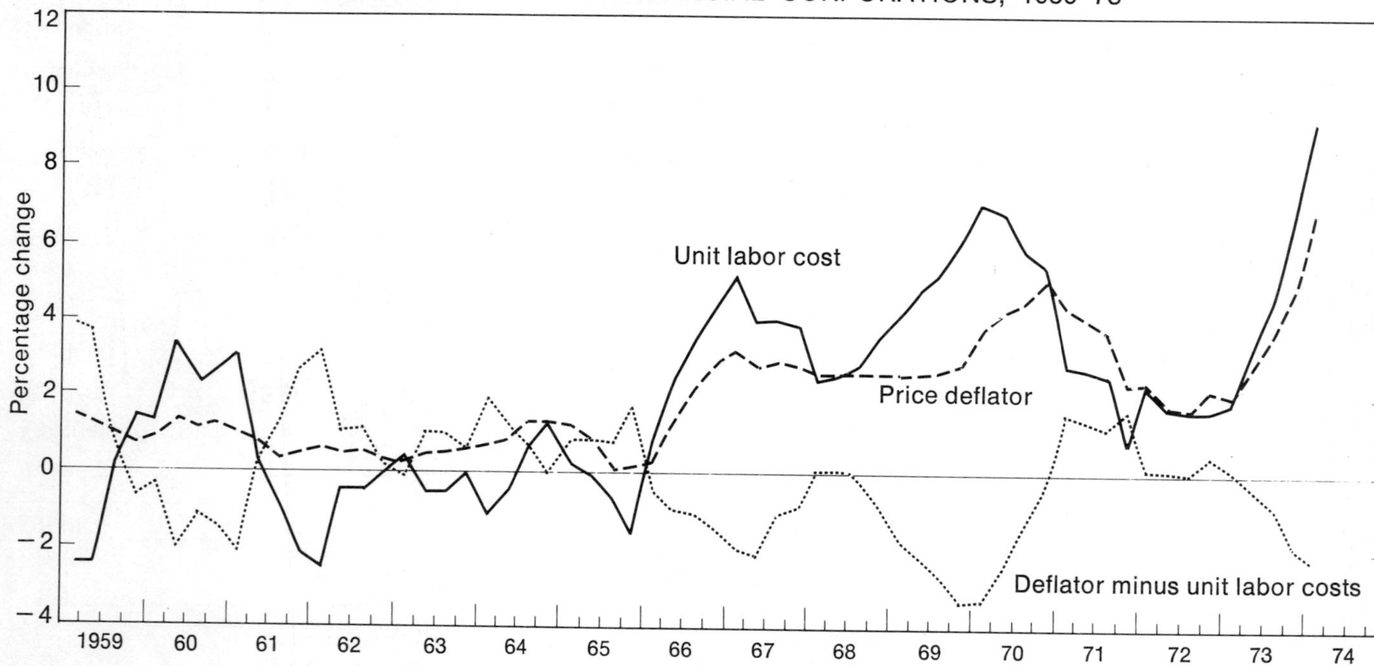

Note: Quarterly percentage changes from four quarters earlier.
Source: U.S. Department of Labor, Bureau of Labor Statistics.

Figure A–2

CHANGES IN PRICE AND UNIT LABOR COSTS AND DIFFERENCE IN CHANGES FOR THE PRIVATE NONFARM SECTOR, 1950–73

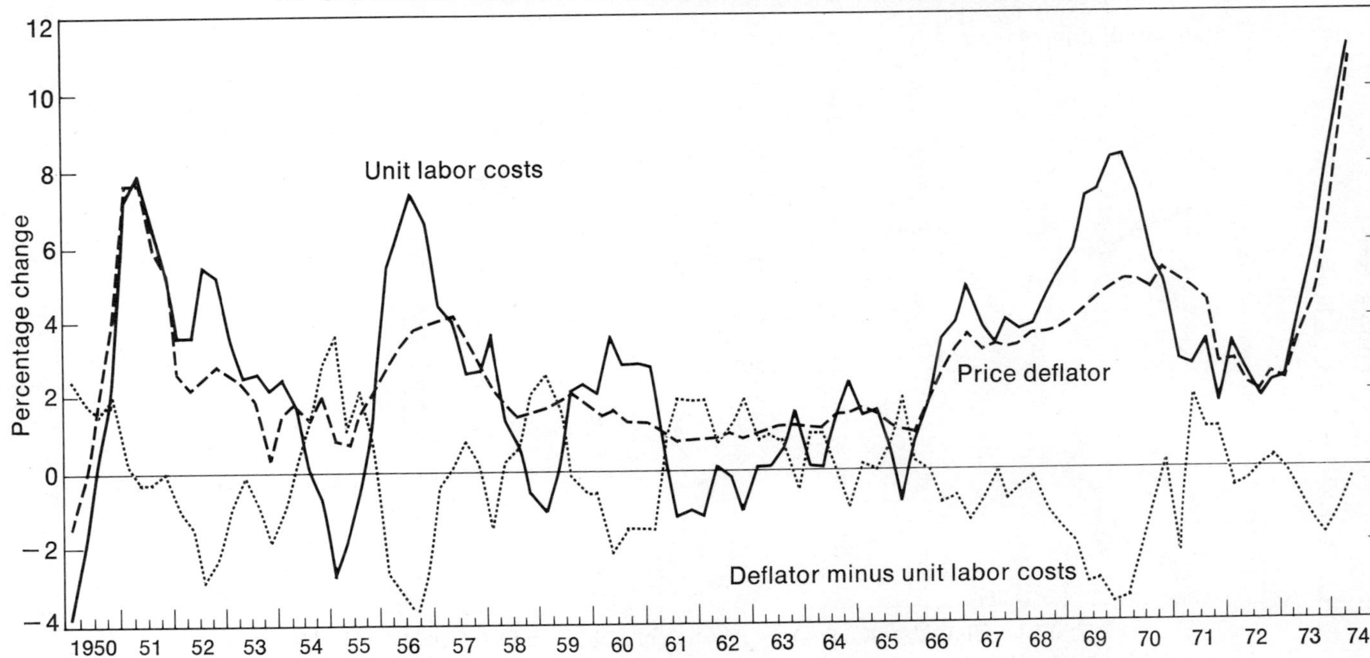

Note: Quarterly percentage changes from four quarters earlier.

Source: U.S. Department of Labor, Bureau of Labor Statistics.

Figure A–3

PRICES OF MAJOR AGRICULTURAL COMMODITIES, 1971–73

$/cwt. **(1) Price of Barrows and Gilts at Omaha, 1971–73**

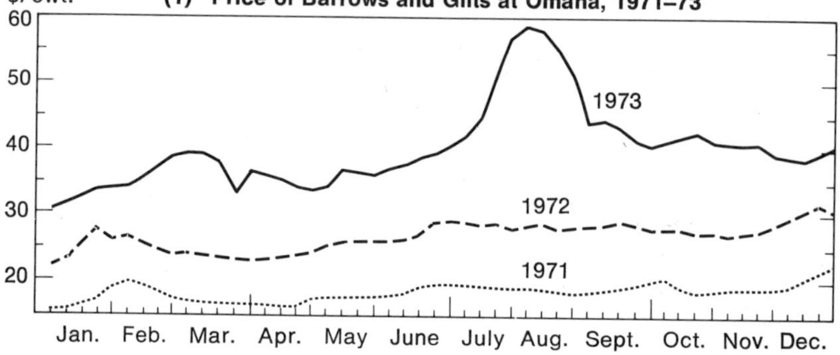

$/cwt. **(2) Price of Choice Feeder Steers* at Omaha, 1971–73**

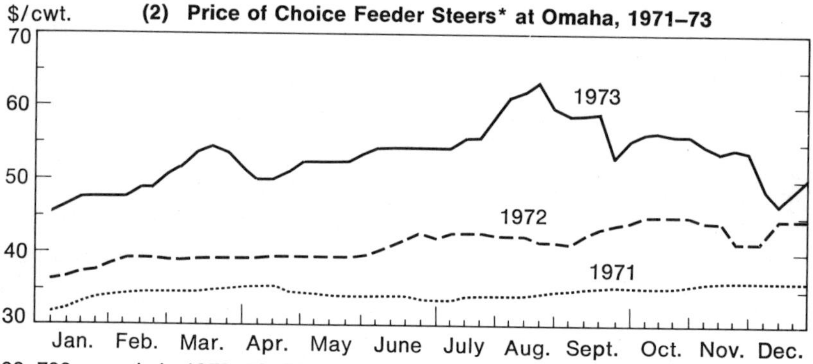

* 600–700 pounds in 1972–73; 550–750 pounds in 1971.

$/cwt. **(3) Price of Choice Slaughter Steers* at Omaha, 1971–73**

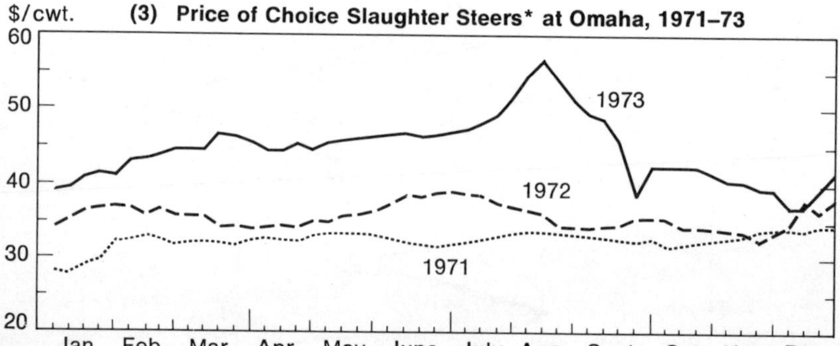

* Sold out of first hands.

Source: U.S. Department of Agriculture, Livestock Division, Agricultural Marketing Service.

Figure A–3 *(continued)*

PRICES OF MAJOR AGRICULTURAL COMMODITIES, 1971–73

(4) Price of Corn at Chicago, 1971–73

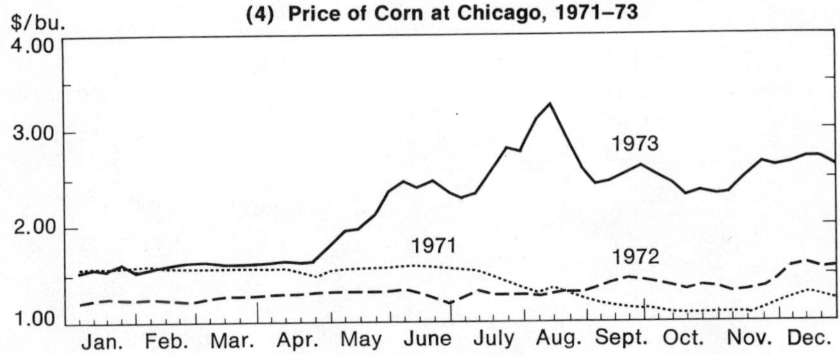

(5) Price of Broilers,* 1971–73

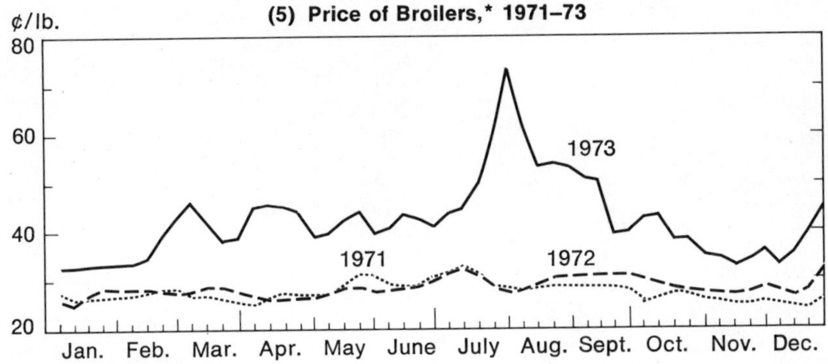

* Nine-city weighted average.

(6) Price of Soybeans at Chicago, 1971–73

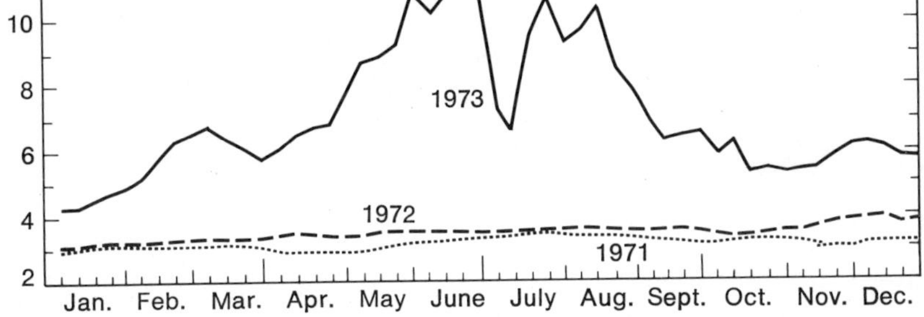

Source: U.S. Department of Agriculture, Economic Research Service.

Cover and book design: Pat Taylor